Zainab Priya

psychologist. Her debut novel *What About Meera* won the inaugural Minara Aziz Hassim Literary Prize in South Africa and was longlisted for both the Etisalat Prize for Fiction (the most prestigious literary prize for African fiction) and the *Sunday Times* Barry Ronge Fiction Prize (South Africa's largest literary award). Her second novel, *The Architecture of Loss*, was shortlisted for the Clara Johnson Award for Women's Literature, 2018. Her short stories were awarded second prize in the Witness True Stories of KwaZulu Natal and she has written opinion pieces for *The New York Times Magazine*, *Marie Claire* and *Elle*. In 2017, she received an Honorary Fellowship in Writing at the International Writers Program at the University of Iowa. She has lived and worked in Dublin and now lives in Durban, South Africa.

What Gandhi Didn't See

BEING INDIAN
IN SOUTH AFRICA

Zainab Priya Dala

SPEAKING
TIGER

SPEAKING TIGER PUBLISHING PVT. LTD
4381/4, Ansari Road, Daryaganj
New Delhi 110002

First published in India by Speaking Tiger in hardback 2018

ISBN: 978-93-88070-53-9
eISBN: 978-93-88070-52-2

10 9 8 7 6 5 4 3 2 1

The moral rights of the author have been asserted.

Typeset in Sabon Roman by SÜRYA, New Delhi
Printed at Sanat Printers, Kundli

To my parents

Contents

Preface 9

What Gandhi Didn't See 31
Growing Up Indian in South Africa

The Safety of Silence 61
Why I Am An Activist

Shades of Brown and Black 75
The New Apartheid Is Money

Canefields vs Casbah: 85
And the Winner Is...Not La La Land

Of Bridal Veils and Monikers 103

Sister Wives 123
Winnie, Phyllis and Jane X

References 149

Preface

When I was about eleven years old, my parents, bothered by my shyness and stuttering, sent me to speech and drama lessons. The lessons were run by a feisty limber South African Indian beauty named Saira Essa. She represented to me everything a woman should be. For my final examinations, which were moderated by a place that sounded very important, although I knew nothing about it—Trinity College—I thought long and hard over what I could do in my spoken word essay. My father, taking keen interest in this new outspoken daughter who had replaced the mumbling fumbling bumbler, took me onto our balcony and pointed. The rows and rows of sugarcane dancing in the fields were all my eye could see.

'Tell them about us. About Indians and how we came here to South Africa,' Dad said.

'But the judges are White people, Daddy,' I protested. 'White people are not interested in hearing stories about people of colour in our country.'

'Tell them anyway.'

My speech began like this (and I still have the handwritten copy):

> 'In 1860, the *SS Truro* and the *SS Belvedere* left the ports of Calcutta and Madras, carrying cargo. This cargo was people. They were the first of a many people that came to South Africa from India to work as indentured labourers on the sugarcane fields.'

At the cue of the word, I brandished a sugarcane stalk, held out in front of me like a weapon. As if showing the judges a thin stalk of undeveloped cane would somehow convince them that this actually happened.

I am looking now at the report that the judges gave me. I got 88 percent. But the criticism was that I was 'too passionate'. Since when is that a criticism?

As the years wore on I promptly forgot all about labourers and sugarcane fields. South Africa had so many other things to think about. South Africans of colour were fighting battles of inequality enforced by a horrific system called apartheid, and thinking about India was the last thing on anyone's mind. Children of my generation were too busy worrying about why we had to study Afrikaans (a South African dialect of Dutch, enforced on our education system), and why we could not go to the White people's beach during summer holidays. India was a foreign, exotic place, and the only 'Indian' we recognised was religious texts which made no sense to us although we were forced to learn them in Sanskrit, and perhaps a few sporadic LPs of Indian movies that some rich person managed to ship home.

Like my peers, I began to become embarrassed about anything remotely Indian. A one-hour slot on a radio station that was allocated to 'Indian content' had us listening secretly to songs from the movie *Amar Akbar Anthony*. If my Dad turned up the volume, I would shout at him to lower it. What if my friends heard it? We baulked at wearing salwar suits to weddings (we called them Punjabis and still do). Women like my mother preferred to wear mini-skirts and I cried for days because I wanted a pair of denims. What was I doing? I wasn't deliberately deleting my lineage. I was simply too ashamed of it, because as an Indian South African girl, it was just better to pretend to be White. Young people of colour saw White people as being far more interesting, more exciting, richer and having much happier lives than us. It translated into a phenomenon that still exists in modern South Africa in 2018, where people of colour still try to mimic the accent of the private-school-educated White folks. We have a funny term for people like them: coconuts—brown on the outside, but white on the inside. Nevertheless, a fair skin was attractive to us brown people, and we often found that the ones who acted, dressed and looked White, were the popular ones.

Now, I have come into my Indianness. Now I can proudly sport a sari or happily play Bollywood songs at full volume. Now I am in my forties, and now I want to know my lineage.

I am not alone in this. The Indian diaspora in South Africa has come full circle. In the last ten years, more and more people are wanting to know where they came from. The ship records of labourers that came from India have only recently been digitised and made accessible to the public. Before this, the records were kept in a dusty documentation centre that no one really wanted to root around in. From those records, I was able to find out that my great-grandfather came to Port Natal, which is now called Durban, from a village near Gorakhpur in Uttar Pradesh. Even those names seem foreign to me. I have visited India as a tourist, spending more time looking for Shah Rukh Khan's house than looking for my village of descent. Each time I visit India, I never feel Indian. I feel more South African than ever, when I stand on a street in Delhi with a bewildered look on my face.

The truth is, I am South African. Everything about my life experience is uniquely South African. I relate more to a Black woman than a woman from India. But, the frustrating thing is that when I am in Durban, I sometimes feel so foreign, that I yearn to be in India. This dichotomy will never leave me. It is a dichotomy that I think almost any immigrant will feel.

I want to be academic and factual in this preface. I want your first introduction to me to encompass all there is to be told about the passage of Indians to South Africa under the Immigration Department Notice dated 17 August 1874. But, I will leave those facts to the historians of indenture, and there are many. I will depart from the things you can find on an internet search or a browse through exhaustively researched history books, and I will do what we as writers are warned never to do—I will personalise history. How can I not? My construct of my own history is formed with the lens of my own reality, my own experiences, rather than the paragraphs in history books. And these essays are simply that: A personal walk in the forest with me through my experiences as a South African woman of Indian descent.

***

It began with indenture. My great-grandfather on my paternal side came here as a labourer. All I know of him is the name the ship log displays, his village and the fact that he had a pockmarked face. He was nineteen years old when he left India. My great-grandmother, if the ship log is anything to go by, was twenty-eight, her village is simply written as 'near Patna' and she had a scar on her inner forearm. That's it. That is all I know. Oral tradition brings up the bodies, a sort-of-life. I hear about apparent fights over a cow, a forbidden love affair, that she was running away from a bad marriage, that he met her on the ship. How much of this it true? Does it even matter? What matters is that three generations down, I am constructing my own reality in a country that tells and then retells its history. It is very frustrating.

As a writer I want to write spanning epics of love and loss. But, maybe, those stories have already been told. My reality did not begin with indenture. My reality began with apartheid. It does not escape me that in both these systems, indenture and apartheid, my reality carries subjugation and tragedy. It is no wonder that I find myself unable to write sweet romantic tales.

Apartheid. We all have heard the term the world over. This is what it is defined as on paper. Apartheid, when translated into English from the original Afrikaans/Dutch means 'Apartness.'

It was a system put in place in South Africa by the White National Party in the year 1948, which allowed for the lawful segregation of people using racial divides. It lawfully prevented equal opportunities for basic human rights to people of colour. It placed White people at the top end of the ladder, giving them legal clout to persecute and subjugate people of colour. It criminalised inter-racial relationships and marriage. It criminalised mixing and mingling of race groups in any way or form.

Mostly, it made it legally impossible for people of colour to have a right to vote or have a say in what happened to them. I grew up under this system. And although my parents, like I believe most immigrant parents do, hid and protected me from it, it was always there.

The racial groups into which people in South Africa were divided under apartheid were, and still are:

White/Caucasian (in which Chinese and Japanese are included); Black people (this includes the indigenous African peoples called Khoi-khoi and San hunter gatherers, the Bantu Black tribes of Zulu, Xhosa, Tswana, Swazi and Ndebele; people of Indian and Pakistani descent, and Coloured people (Coloured here refers to an actual official population group of mixed race/mulatto people who gained this title of 'coloured' in the nineteenth century in South Africa). Apartheid made laws that forced the different racial groups to live separately and have separate, and unequal, access to basic amenities such as housing, education and employment. Such laws included:

- The Population Registration Act of 1950 which made it legally binding for all

citizens to register under a designated
population group.

- The Immorality and Prohibiton of Mixed
  Marriages Act (1949 and 1950) which
  legally prohibited races to mix as friends,
  lovers or enter into marriages across race.
- The Group Areas Act (1950) which legally
  enforced Indian, Black and Coloured
  groups to live in segregated areas and not
  be allowed to enter Whites Only areas,
  except during designated times, when they
  went to work in White people's homes or
  hotels, for example, after which curfew
  was imposed. Breaking that curfew was
  punishable by imprisonment.

Once these laws were placed and enforced, apartheid
became a social system which severely disadvantaged
the majority of the population because of skin colour
and dehumanised a large majority of the people of
South Africa.

It is a sensitive debate in South Africa as to how
the White minority achieved such power as to rule
over the majority of the population.

The indigenous peoples of the southern tip of
Africa are the nomadic San and Khoi people. White

South Africans are primarily people of Dutch (known as Afrikaaners) and British origins. In 1652, the Dutch East India Company established a permanent 'refreshment' station at the Cape of Good Hope. They arrived with arms and gifts, and began a bartering system with the native people of the Cape, and eventually took over much of the fertile resources and land. The British arrived in South Africa in the 1920s and although the British and the Dutch were both considered Caucasian, they were on opposing sides that fought for supremacy. After the two Anglo-Boer Wars (Boer is an Afrikaans term for Dutch farmer), a treaty was announced between the British and the Dutch. The National Party which was primarily a Dutch party, was eventually voted into power after the treaty. In the Nationalist Agenda was the law of apartheid.

In the system of apartheid, its most devious methodology was giving equality in increments. The ruling White party knew that divisions in the smallest of acts would result in fracturing a large majority of the people of colour. Here's how they did it:

People of colour were divided into:

1. Indians (that's me—a person of Indian descent).

2. Coloureds. As explained above, the Coloured community comprises a mixture of mainly Black Africans with White settlers. The White settlers include the Dutch, French and British who settled in South Africa. As Indians began to arrive in South Africa, and most especially after the Immorality Act had been abolished, some people of Indian descent married and/ or had children with White Caucasians, Black Africans and Coloured peoples. The children of these unions were mulatto (mixed race) in theory, but they often took the paternal population designation. One atrocious method used to place a person of mixed race in a population group was called 'the pencil test'. Here, a pencil was inserted into the person's hair, and if their hair was straight, the pencil fell out, thus allowing them to identify as White (if they were fair-skinned) or Coloured (mulatto). If the pencil remained in their Afro-style hair, they had to register as Black African. There are many recorded cases of siblings who underwent the pencil test, and were separated based on differing results.

3. Chinese and other Asians who were legally considered White.
4. Black Africans, as explained above.

So, even today when I apply for a bank loan, I have to check one of those boxes. There is a new box they've recently introduced for 'Others'. I have yet to check that one.

When the White government created apartheid they also ensured that the basic amenities of life were given in tiny increments to some groups whilst others were ignored. Mainly, and perhaps only, the Black population was ignored. People of Indian descent were given better places to live with significantly better facilities like sanitation, water and schools. These places were terrible box-like townships in arid terrain, but they were better than nothing. The Indians who had come to South Africa as traders had money, so they lived in their own houses and apartments surrounding their businesses. This created a further divide—between Indians of the indentured class, and trader Indians. It was unequal, but some people were more unequal than others.

I know I have been brought up in relative privilege compared to a Black woman of my age. I had a comfortable home, safety and schooling. But, that comfort for me always felt uncomfortable. I could never fully actualise how I could complain about 'the White Man' as all my peers used to, when this White Man was doing worse things to the Black people that lived around me. Whilst my peers and I enjoyed this upper level of inequality, there were many among us who didn't like it as much as we should. My parents were vehement about one thing, and that was keeping me away from getting involved in the struggle against apartheid. And I would never say my involvement was even a tiny smidge of real activism. If I were to describe myself as an activist I would do it with the reservation of an imposter. Because, I was not an activist in its true raw sense back then. When I was growing up, my acts of resistance came by fighting my parents. Every teenager does that. I was not unique. I fought them to tell me the truths. I fought them to allow me to make a choice about whether I could be 'too passionate'. I fought them to free me. It was incidental, perhaps accidental that everything I was fighting my parents to allow me to do ended up being a fight for equality. Now, I am an activist. But I don't confine my work to fighting racial injustice. Now, I get passionate about any injustice.

I came from a community that lived like frightened little ant colonies. Stay as silent and invisible as possible and you'll just slip through the cracks. I was silent for a long while, fearful of being ostracised. But, when I entered university and the country was at its height of the fight against apartheid in the early 90s, I catapulted myself out of the comfort zone. Yes, the ostracising did come, and I still live with it. I am not a silent smiling wife, hosting tea parties. Nor do I shout from the rooftops every chance I get. But, I write. That is my activism. I write the things most people want to hide.

In these essays I try to bring this little colony out by using my own personal experiences of being an Indian woman in South Africa as a lens. After South Africa won the massive struggle for democracy and abolished apartheid in 1994, there has been a mad dash for ownership of some kind. People are scrambling around like ants whose safe home was broken, and although we are largely aware that the safety of that home was actually not very safe at all, it was built on a foundation of inequality, as a very young democracy we are now trying to find out who we are and where we fit in. The place most people are going to in this scrabble is to their lineage. It is not only South African Indians that are finally accessing ship logs, creating WhatsApp groups and Facebook pages that talk about tales of the Girmitiyas,* all other race groups as well are searching for their defining roots.

In the context of myself and the people I surround myself with within the South African Indian diaspora, we veer between identifying with a Bollywood-type India, and an India of the 1800s. Much of what is India escapes us, yet we know that it is there. We want more. In this search, we troubleshoot to Bollywood with the occasional slant towards what we deem 'cultural exchange' whenever an Indian sitarist or santoor maestro graces our shores for concerts that are often lost on most of the listeners. Yet, though they may not know the difference between the alaap of Raga Bhairav from the jhala of Raga Jhinjhoti, many SA Indians enjoy music from India that may not necessarily be Bollywood. Kathak and Bharatnatyam are gaining popularity as dance forms

---

*Girmitiyas was a term coined for the indentured labourers. It refers to the word 'agreement' which was the document signed by labourers who were indentured from India. In their pronunciation, the document became known as a 'Girmit,' and those that took up indenture were called Girmitiyas.

for young SA Indians to learn and perfect. Now, people as old as eighty are going to Hindi or Tamil school, and Qawali is a very popular item on the social agenda. Now, so eager are we for anything Indian, that any art, culture, music or fashion from India is replacing the great dream to be White.

Let's put it this way, in dance clubs now, the young kids can be heard calling each other 'yaar' and 'faltu' more often than they call each other 'dude' and 'useless,' when they are drunk enough to joke around.

We just cannot grab hold of the reality, and often we wonder if we ought to be doing so in the first place. Suddenly, we find that SA Indians are becoming victims of affirmative action and Black economic empowerment. Our biggest issue now is trying to say to the burgeoning Black middle class that we are one of them, and when a few troublesome elements tell us to 'go back to India', we know that we can never quite do that. Home is South Africa, and although we sometimes get frightened and insecure about where we fit in, most of us are positive that we do fit in.

South Africa has recently seen some dark days. The ex-President Jacob Zuma was found to be colluding with a group of businessmen from India who settled in South Africa and began a rapid and very corrupt process of State Capture. These brothers, along with President Zuma and his son, took over the governmental departments that supplied electricity to the entire country, transport systems, banking, and had their fingers in almost every government-run system. Corrupt tender processes and the disappearance of millions into private coffers saw South Africa reach junk status in 2017. They even had a hand in deciding who our finance minister would be, and it is alleged that they would host large parties at their palatial home in Saxonwold, Johannesburg, offering ministerial positions to those that colluded with them. The result of this on a ground level was that every person who remotely looked like an Indian, including Indian-descent South Africans whose families had fought the apartheid system, was being typecast. 'Go back to India' became a clarion call that terrified us all. The queue line for many SA Indians to get their PIO cards or emigrate to New Zealand suddenly became very long. But, there are those who refused to take the exit strategy.

The people organised a call to resistance. It

hearkened back to the days when the people marched the streets and ousted apartheid. Now, in marches across the land, protests and rallies, South Africans of every colour called for the law to step in. The result was that President Zuma and his corrupt friends were ousted out. We have a new man in the hot seat, President Cyril Ramaphosa, and we are all waiting to see if he is, as some call him, 'a Mandela Man'.

This is South Africa today. It is frustrating as much as it is beautiful. We fight like siblings across the dinner table. Every now and then a rant on social media sends people into a racial frenzy and the 'us and them' rhetoric mill grinds. But soon, it ends, and our attention is taken by British royal weddings, soccer and Trevor Noah in New York. As Indian-descended people in South Africa, we fight over why a radio station plays more Hindi songs than Tamil. We all go dizzy when a singing star from Bollywood comes for a concert tour. We aggregate in small groups and recite Urdu verse to each other over delicious dishes cooked by the many Pakistani nationals whom we have welcomed into our world. The most amazing fusion dance productions featuring traditional Zulu dance with Kathak hold sway. Bhojpuri is no longer a cringe-worthy dialect we hide, but now plays and radio shows are produced in it. A threat of malicious anger riles up Blacks against Indians; shopkeepers who don't pay well and housewives who only allow their Black domestic workers to drink from separate enamel cups becomes a burning conversation for what seems like eternity. Crime is horrific, the Indians are soft targets, the newspapers say. But, this is our life and our country. I have loved my place in this country. My activism now extends towards issues of patriarchy and that has nothing to do with colour. I know that wherever you go, if you tell people you are from South Africa, they immediately ask about apartheid and race. The thing is, South Africa is rapidly moving towards conversations that are not even about that typecasting. There is a whole South Africa that no longer engages in indentured or slavery or apartheid discourse. I fear that, like all those of this middling generation of people 'not old enough to truly know apartheid but not young enough to be born free of it', I am still stuck in those conversations, and I need to catch up. I do know that those conversations needed to happen as we South African Indians now prepare ourselves for new ones.

I have to admit, lately I have become very scared. There seems to be a virulent anti SA Indian wave amongst certain parties in the Black Majority, such as the Economic Freedom Fighters who wear red berets and bow down to Marxist principles, but also wear expensive Breitling watches which they hide under rough cuffs. The leader, Julius Malema, an intimidating figure with a very loud mouth and a knowledge of Marx, Lenin and the South African law, has been howling rhetoric that the 'majority of Indians in South Africa are racist' towards Blacks, and treat Blacks badly.

The result of this vitriol has been a wave of fear and racism across the country that has Indian people who fought hard in the struggle for democracy having to defend themselves and their right to land, to be recognised as South Africans and more hurtfully, to proclaim their non-racism. Julius Malema and his party have not wasted any time in bringing the issue of Mahatma Gandhi forward as argument, stating boldly that Gandhi loved the British, was racist, colour-conscious, believed that Black people are inferior and enjoyed the privilege of being an upper caste, rich Gujarati Indian. For the Gandhis, Guptas and certain other allegedly racist names they dig up, we retaliate screaming the names of the late Comrades Ahmed Timol (the first person to die under police detention whilst fighting apartheid), Ahmed Kathrada, or Uncle Kathy, as we affectionately call him, who was imprisoned as long as Nelson Mandela on Robben Island, Dr Kesavalu Goonam, Phyllis Naidoo, Monty Naicker, Yusuf Dadoo, Fatima and Ismail Meer, and the list goes on.

But, the fear is still there. The words that paint SA Indians as racist have resulted in a reverse racism towards SA Indians in schools, streets and subtle spaces. In looking for a place we can call home, we look at Africa. I want to know that Africa looks at us too.

FIRST SUGAR MILL
IN SOUTH AFRICA

What Gandhi Didn't See
Growing Up Indian in South Africa

I am a fourth-generation Indian in South Africa, which makes me a South African of Indian descent. Indians arrived in South Africa in the 1860s from the ports of Calcutta and Madras after being recruited (or kidnapped) from remote villages. They came to work as indentured labour on the sugarcane plantations, much like the diaspora that went to Mauritius, Suriname, Trinidad, Fiji and Guyana.

In their agreement of indenture, Indians were promised a free passage back to India after five years of labour. Many were unable to secure their passage home for reasons that were financial or sociological, or both. Many were re-indentured in order to earn a living. My great-grandfather was one of them.

Though he was eventually able to pay his way out of indenture, he died soon after and could never return to India. His son, my grandfather, worked as a bricklayer and saved enough money to buy ten acres of farmland to plant sugarcane. It took him over two decades to pay for the land, but he did eventually become a landowner and a successful entrepreneur. In the process, he was never able to return with his family to India. He decided to remain in South Africa, and make the farm his home and his legacy.

The sugarcane farm was called iMona. The farmhouse, with its twelve bedrooms that surrounded an inner courtyard, sat on a hill, and spreading below it like the pleats in a saree, were the ten acres of farmland. I was born on this farm, and spent the early years of my life amongst the people, the animals and the natural wonder of fields and a gurgling stream. Every harvesting season we would burn the sugarcane so that these burnt sickly sweet stalks could be taken to the mill to be ground and processed.

The loud shouts of my cousins and I echoing in the fields as we bravely tried to outrun a fire ring out in my dreams sometimes. My own children would never know this visceral call to our heritage: 'Aag aati hai!' The sound of a hundred children's voices and the crackling spit of fire. We had no fear. We ran, we fell, we felt tiny burns on our skin from spitting embers. These were our medals, and our happiest times.

Somehow, I knew that there was a sugar mill somewhere. I knew that the smell of burnt raw sugar permeated everything from your clothes to your schoolbooks. Often, on walks with my father, we would see in the distance beyond the fields, clouds of smoke billowing upwards from tall turrets. I never visited the sugar mill, which was the largest and most historical one in South Africa, owned by the Moreland Sugar Company, or as we called it—Tongaat Huletts. Every person who hailed from Tongaat learned the name Hulett before we learned our own properly. The sugar baron family had been the lineage point of almost all of us. From primary school to the rebellion of high school, we all knew someone who had worked on those fields or in those white Dutch-style buildings, carrying tea trays or sweeping floors.

I don't think any of us questioned why we lived in this town steeped in so much history, yet we were not allowed to learn that history. We were taken on school field trips to Durban to visit silly miniature versions of the city enclosed by a fence—a place called Mini Town—and we were allowed to enter the Natural Science Museum at City Hall, in journeys that took most of the day. Yet, not once were we taken on a ten-minute bus ride to the vanguard of our own town—the Tongaat Hulett Sugar Company and Sugar Mill. They hid us from it. Those teachers and parents. Or maybe, our starched white uniforms and poor shoes were not welcome in those halls. The large brown-button eyes of a hundred descendants of the people whose sweat had built that town were not allowed to see any of its reality. It was unfair.

I, much like my friends and cousins, went through life in Tongaat with blinkers on, not looking at the smoke that rose and still rises from the sugar mill. My life was peppered with mild annoyances, like the black dust that burning sugarcane leaves on clothes. My mother, who came from the big city of Durban, and who had driven a car, worn bell-bottoms and been on cruise ships and motorcycles, would swing between states of protecting me from knowing about my paternal heritage, and telling me about it. She would infuse me with Cliff Richard songs and stories about how her mother had nicknamed her twin brother and her Georgie and Bertie (the two British royal princes). And then there were those times that she would talk of with fondness, of falling in love with the sugarcane fields and the old farm school that she taught in, and how much she had enjoyed hearing stories of the labourers that my grandfather told her. Her open communication, in all its dichotomy, was a welcome balm to the silence of my father.

My father, a third-generation non-resident Indian, whose grandfather had come from a village near Gorakhpur in Uttar Pradesh, preferred not to talk much about his heritage. But, things changed when he reached sixty years of age. Why? I will never know. But what I do know is that everything about my heritage from my paternal side had been spoken of by others, including my father's brothers and sisters, not him. Maybe, he suffered the affliction of a love marriage to a woman who was seen as superior to him, and he wanted to delete his inferiority in the eyes of his children. But, I am seeing now how I also do the similar thing to my children. My husband, like my mother, comes from the big city of Durban, and his heritage is one of the Muslim business class that came to South Africa long after the indentured labourers* and anyway, let me just say it—he is considered higher class than I am, so we tend to appropriate this onto our children. Perhaps my father had done the same for many years. And, perhaps he decided to speak openly about our mixed-up heritage only after my sister and I were safely and happily stowed away into good marriages. Things are sometimes as ugly as that. But speak he did. It became a river that never stopped. One day a year ago we were at a fancy dinner party held by my cousin from my mother's side of the family—a very rich and successful doctor amongst a family of doctors. He lived in an area we still call today a White Area, which means that before 1994, none of us would have ever dreamed of walking past a house there, let alone living in one. My father was quiet during this dinner, but perhaps a few glasses of expensive whiskey loosened his tongue, and he started talking

---

*Over 100,000 Indians arrived as slaves from the subcontinent in 1684 and lived in Cape Town. The first Indian indentured labourers arrived on 16 November 1860. The passenger/trader Indians began arriving around 1875 to meet the need for commercial trade in the community, Black and Indian as well as Coloured.

about his childhood on the farm. My mother tried to quieten him, not because she was ashamed, but because she knew he was about to cry. The room went silent as if a spell had been cast by a mournful farm-accented voice ringing out among the posh 'White' accents of my cousins and his friends. But, minutes into his monologue, my cousin's husband blurted: 'Oh really now, Babs, should we get you an audition for another 'Coolie Odyssey'?' ('The Coolie Odyssey' was a play on the indentured labourers written, directed by, and starring, Rajesh Gopie, a South African Indian dramatist).

My father fell into silence, and my husband, who is sensitive to the point of extreme protection of my father at most times, ushered him outside. I was carrying my baby son, and looking at these two men, standing next to a Balinese-inspired swimming pool, sharing a cigarette and probably chatting about the price of fuel, it was not lost on me that I was carrying in my arms the actual reality of a class divide. My son will always have to negotiate this divide and there is nothing I can do to protect him from it. Why would I need to protect him? Well, to put it as succinctly as I can, in South Africa, we let go of the caste system in the bowels of a ship in the

1800s, but we adopted a system that became very insidious. Fellow writers and historians, Ashwin Desai and Goolam Vahed, in their detailed opus, *Inside Indenture: A South African Story, 1860–1914*, describe these people who dropped their caste into the Indian Ocean as 'twice-born'. Here, they refer to the fact that in the shiphold, there was no room for caste or class. An Indian inside there was an Indian who ate and slept alongside all others. But once they arrived at the port, and the documents of demographics were being created, a lower caste could easily take himself up a few notches. Today, in contemporary South Africa, caste is obsolete. We all know enough by now to question the Maharaja and Singh surname with a studied eye for actual refinement in behaviour, language and of course, education. This does not mean there are no divisions. The divisions go deep. They are based on religion, economics, language and colour. Of course, I know that these divisions are changeable ones—much like dropping your caste at a shipyard, now you can change your religion, think and grow rich, lighten your skin and perfect your English. This malleability scares the ones who wielded class like gold crowns. I admit, my maternal family and my husband's family are those who did. They are forgiven because they didn't know they were doing it.

In South Africa, the business class came to the shores of Natal mainly from the villages of Gujarat. My father-in-law describes it well when he tells me in thick Gujarati: 'One side of the street is Muslim Desai family. Opposite side of street is Hindu Desai family. Both Desais understand each other and get along better than even Muslim Urdu speakers or Calcuttiah people.'

I don't look at anything he is saying as derogatory. The reason is that he is not insulting anyone, he is simply stating facts. The Gujarati community aggregated together in a code of business and called each other 'Aapra-wallahs'. They still use this term today. An acquaintance, who is a great-grandson of Mahatma Gandhi, once came over to my house to collect items I wanted to donate to a family rendered homeless after a fire. I had known him for some years, and had interacted with him many times on charitable or literary correspondence. But, within minutes of the mutual spotting of an Aapra-wallah in the room, I ceased to exist in the conversation. My husband, a Muslim, and my associate, a Hindu, both spoke Gujarati that went far above my head. I had learned the basics of the language, to communicate with my husband's family who spoke only Gujarati. My mother's family were too high class to speak any vernacular, and only the Queen's English would do. My father's family spoke a combination of Urdu, Hindi and Bhojpuri. My best friend spoke Afrikaans and the children I grew up playing with spoke Zulu. Add to this mix the terms that each of us reserved for each grouping, which are as derogatory as being called Coolies, and it is no wonder that I cannot sleep some nights.

Indians who left as indentured labourers from the port of Calcutta are called Calcuttiahs, and Indians who left as indentured labourers from the port of Madras are called Madrasis. The Muslim community have their own lines of division and I find that these lines are deeply hurtful. Muslims who arrived in South Africa as indentured labourers are thought to come from Hyderabad. Although many chroniclers say that the majority of the Muslim community in South Africa who are not business arrivals are actually converts to Islam. This is how the Muslim community divide their people—colour and language. It used to be money, but now everyone is keeping up with the Joneses and the famous Gujarati Trust

Funds* are running on empty, having cossetted very large and extravagant families for two generations.

The Memon Muslim community is a very small one, but wields a large economic clout. The Memoni Muslims are known to have come from different areas around India, originally from Kathiawar, but finally settled as a community near Porbandar in Gujarat, from where a number of them migrated to South Africa as traders and businessmen. Another batch of Gujarati Muslims came from different villages in Gujarat, and left for South Africa from the port of Surat. They proudly refer to each other as Surtis and use the term 'Hedroo', to describe any other Muslim who is not Gujarati or Memoni. Hedroos, a bastardisation of Hyderabadi, is used to speak of the class of Muslims whom the Surti community look upon as low class and poor. Inter-marriages between Surtis and Hedroos are still frowned upon. I am reminded of my own wedding day, when my

---

*Gujarati Trust Funds were set up from the mid-1870s by wealthy Gujarati families, to cater for all educational, medical and housing needs of their community. When Gandhi arrived in South Africa, the Gandhi Trust was set up to cater for legal and charitable needs and to publish a newspaper called *The Indian Opinion*.

husband's aunt told me that in the history of the Dala family, it was the first time they had accepted a 'mixed' girl for any of their boys. Their bloodline had remained pure Surti Gujarati till 2006, the year of my nikkah. I responded to the aunt by a small nod that day, and replied to her: 'Hahn ji.'

Much like the twice-born that Desai and Vahed refer to in their book, I am a twice-born too. I seem to have unknowingly (or perhaps for peace) deleted my Urdu-Bhojpuri-Hindu paternal history. I deleted my Hindu identity to be reborn as Muslim and most of my life is spent trying to ignore that there is any part of me that is even remotely Hindu. I have done this because it is just easier when one is married into a 'pure' Muslim family, who also ignore any sign of my Hindu identity and upbringing. I secretly long for the days on our farm in iMona when all of us would gather in our large courtyard, the Indians—both Hindu and Muslim—and learn songs. I think the sound of the azaan evokes a squeezing of my heart as much as the chorus of 'Raghupati Raaghav Raja Ram'. I recall singing the verse 'Ishwar Allah tero naam,' very vociferously. I often long for Priya, yet I answer to the name Zainab. When people ask me whether to call me Zainab or Priya, I always hesitate.

I still don't know which name to use. Each name is associated with a religion, and each religion is associated with a different time in my life. I was very happy as a farm girl called Priya. I am functionally happy as a wife and mother called Zainab.

* * *

The bhajan 'Raghupati Raaghav' brings me to think deeply about Gandhi. But more than the bhajan, Gandhi has been on my mind for a few weeks now because I have been contacted by a French radio journalist who is coming to South Africa to do a piece on Gandhi in this country and she has selected Ashwin Desai and myself to speak to. In her emails, she asks me to take her to places that are important to me, that Gandhi has had an influence on. I am stumped. Wind knocked out of my sails. I refuse twice. She persists. I finally agree, but with trepidation. I am about to be exposed to the entire world. I turn to my father, like I always do in times when I am lost for words, when his words sometimes become my own.

Over a telephone line that sounds echoey, he recites textbook excerpts of Gandhi's autobiography,

The Story of My Experiments with Truth. Our conversation goes like this:

> Dad: 'Oh, he was a great man, a great man. Have you read his autobiography?'
>
> Me: 'Yes, but Dad...that is not what I am asking you. I want to know how much of him did you know as a child growing up in Tongaat? Did my Dada ever talk about him? Did you guys study him? Was he part of your conversation growing up?'
>
> Dad: 'No. No, he wasn't. But read his autobiography, Priya, he was a great man.'
>
> Me: 'I read it.'
>
> Dad: 'So...what do you want to know from me?'
>
> Me: 'Well, the truth is Dad, I hate to admit it but the first time I ever realised there was a person called MK Gandhi was when we watched that Attenborough movie. Growing up, we never really had any access to information about him.'
>
> Dad: 'Yes, well that is the fault of the White Man. He only allowed certain things in history books. Take it from me, I studied history even in university and all we were allowed to learn was about Vasco da Gama, Jan van Riebeeck and Dick King. Forget Gandhi, Mandela all that.'

Me: 'I know that, Dad. Which is why I am trying to get a personal account of Gandhi into my frame of reference for this French journalist. I can't just spend her time and mine reciting parts of his autobiography. She can do that herself. She wants to know *my* Gandhi.'

Silence.

Dad: 'Fine. Bring her home to Tongaat. I will talk to her.'

Me: 'You sure about that?'

Dad: 'I said bring her. So bring her.'

I bring her. She is anxious and ready for a taped conversation and all she wants to hear about is Gandhi. She has stayed at his swish yoga-massage-spa Satyagraha House in Johannesburg, which was Gandhi's place to stay when he was in South Africa. She regales me with stories about how she looked at his belongings and his books and that the place had four and a half stars on TripAdvisor. I just drive through the sugarcane fields and hope my Dad knows what he is going to say. Because it is true, I don't know much about Gandhi that either you or I couldn't find in any history book. Growing up, we never really spoke about him. My school friends will attest to it, we knew *of* him. We knew about how he came to South Africa as a barrister to fight a case of a Memon business family from Porbandar who had settled in South Africa and how he was thrown off a train in a town near Durban, called Pietermaritzburg. In fact, as I write this essay, the Indian High Commission in South Africa is holding a fancy dinner and press conference about the celebrations that will commemorate 125 years of that historic train eviction. I know people who have been invited to this press conference. Mainly they are business people and entertainment celebrities. I doubt my aunt sitting in her farmhouse in Tongaat even knows such a press conference ever happened, let alone any knowledge of what is being commemorated. Because, here is my experiment with truth: Gandhi was never important in my upbringing. I cannot hide from this. I can tell you all the books I have read about him and by him, I can tell you that it is now a great fashion to know about Gandhi and throw around Gandhian quotes and misquotes much like the fashion of Rumi quotes that float on top of blue lakes as memes circulated amongst the aspirant-enlightened, but I can't say that Gandhi ever knew what was happening on the farm of my birth.

In school, we were never taken to see the station where he was thrown out of the train compartment, in as much obliteration as we never saw the sugar mill. But this sugar mill will now haunt me and I sometimes wish that French journalist had not come along and I had not opened the floodgates with my father. He actually ignores every single question the journalist asks him about Gandhi. Instead, when we settle into the car after some tea in china cups from my mother's best tea set, my father instructs me to drive to Compensation.

'What? Dad, why do you want to go there? Compensation of all places?'

I have reason to wonder. The place with this vile name 'Compensation' (which is its official name on any Google Map), is a place near Tongaat which has nothing much to offer. Growing up, we knew some children who came from that area and they were the poor ones, the terribly poor ones, the ones whose fathers swept streets. Now, I think of them as the best ones. But, although we could never articulate why, Compensation, a place ten minutes' drive from my home, was always avoided. I think my father had had enough of avoiding his history. The French journalist just provided him with the perfect reason to show it to me. And Gandhi had nothing to do with this conversation.

What happened when we got there was, we broke in. We literally took a rock and broke a lock that could as easily be broken with a toe, it was that rusted and it was that flimsy. My father, the journalist, her translator and me. We broke into the first sugar mill in South Africa, the Edmund Morewood Sugar Mill, established in 1850. The place was eerie, overgrown with foliage and hanging vines that looked Gothic against the cement structures which met our eyes. I felt my skin crawl and I thought it was perhaps that we had stepped out of bright sunshine into this gloom, but it was much more. All of us were silent, on instinct we knew there was a presence there—a history that no book would ever speak about in all its complexity. Stepping through the long grass, afraid of black mambas which flourished in that area but aching to see everything, I walked towards a stone structure.

I saw two pillars that stood straight up, deeply embedded in the earth. Rusted ring hinges indicated that there were things that could have been attached to those two pillars. The floor now mossy and covered in plants that we as children called devil's thorn, was a wide circle recessed into the ground. In the centre was a stone structure, with even more rusted red hinges made of the cast iron circles you see on medieval castles in popular television mini-series. Except these were the real thing. Leading from the circle, a thickly dug concrete trough fractured the earth and ran downhill for a few metres into a huge stone trough. And that was it. That was the first sugar mill in South Africa. Nothing of machinery or pulleys and levers in there. Nothing. But human machinery.

'See this,' my father almost pulled me into that recessed circle. I didn't resist.

'I don't get it,' I told him.

Both of us had forgotten the journalist was even with us. This was our conversation. And it was very long overdue.

He proceeded to explain to me how the stone structure in the centre, now crumbling was the remnants of three concrete barrels placed next to each other, and that the rusted hinges were attachments to wooden beams. The top of each of the three barrels had a large circular concrete barrel, now absent, which was attached to two long wooden arms. I probably looked like I was confused so he took a stick and drew a sketch of what he meant in the hard dry earth. It looked rudimentary and certainly nothing I would imagine a grand Mr Morewood would have designed as an entry point for an entire diaspora to be brought to across the dark waters.

It was the French journalist who asked the question: 'So was it mules that walked in the circle, with the wooden poles to turn that crusher?'

'No. Not mules,' Dad said. And we all understood. It was people. Labourers. Indentured shoulders and backs, breaking as they crushed and crushed sugarcane. The sweet juice ran down the trough and into the pond-like well. I gulped down a bitterness. My own great-grandfather had been a labourer for the Moreland Sugar Mill. Where I stood was possibly the place where he had walked around and around in a never-ending circle, like a mule. I knew then, the years of my father's silence. I know it now also because it is an odyssey that most people will never know about, and now as well, I find it difficult to talk about.

My father looked at the journalist and both she and I looked like we were ready to flee that place, that eerie piece of my own history.

'So, you want to talk to me about Gandhi, yes?

Well, Gandhi was a great man. But he never came here, did he? He came to Tongaat to visit a big business family there to collect money for the Natal Indian Congress. Yes, he fought the White Man, he printed newspapers, he held meetings. But he never came here, did he? My grandfather, Sewpersad Dukhan and his wife Nunkie were too busy staying alive and not being beaten to death to attend meetings about Congresses. My father could not read. What would he do with a newspaper called *The Indian Opinion*? But, Gandhi was a great man.'

Both the journalist and I appeared confused. Was my father maligning Gandhi, or was he simply stating the truth? I didn't ask him the question there, as I could tell he was emotional, but I hearkened back to his advice to read the books he himself had gifted me, one on my thirtieth birthday and one when I turned forty. The former was Gandhi's autobiography, *The Story of My Experiments with Truth*. And the latter was a whopping 1248-page opus of extracts of Gandhi's own letters and writings, edited by Fatima Meer, and contributed to in part by my friend, Advocate Hassim Seedat. I have scant been able to get through this entire book entitled *The South African Gandhi: An Abstract of the Speeches and Writings of MK Gandhi*, and often wondered if my Dad should have rather gifted me a customary handbag or perfume instead. I allowed my Dad his moments of rumination, not pressing the issue further. I would peer into the books in my late night hours, that I knew.

Dad stopped talking and began to leave the sugar mill back through that broken chain fence we had stolen in through. In the car, he told me to hang a left at the place where the gravel road becomes smooth tar. We stopped for coffee at a tourist attraction. The Edmund Morewood Memorial Gardens was manicured and beautiful, nothing like the tangle of weeds and vines of the sugar mill that bore his name as well. A large concrete slab covered by planters filled with perfect purple pansies and ferns beckoned us with a plaque that told us the slab was placed to cover the pond that sugarcane juice would be stored in. Again, a deletion in history. Again, a cover-up.

* * *

I know that the French journalist did not run the story, or at least any part of my time with her. I know this because my Dad and I didn't tell her anything that she wanted to hear. We told her our truth, and that is that MK Gandhi began the makings into a Mahatma in South Africa. He had evolved from believing in the divisions between Blacks and Indians, and the divisions between classes. He had known more about the business class than the labourers, and had begun his early years believing in a caste system. But he had evolved and it was his intervention that saw the prohibition of the atrocious acts of indenture finally in 1911. His resistance campaign had begun the earliest forms of equality fights in a country that ran with deep racism. I forgot all about the French journalist when later that night I could not sleep. I dug through those two books like I was hunting for a reason to understand the man who was called a Mahatma. I was still struck by a dichotomy, that of my own personal sense of angst as to whether Gandhi had really reached the masses of the poverty-stricken indentured people in the farms, people like my own family, and the fact that he indeed did fight for them on a macro level.

My epiphany did not come in the pages of books. I read in his autobiography about how he lamented that he was unable to really reach the people of Tongaat and Stanger, and that he did indeed go there for fund-raising, but it was a necessary step. One particular line jumps out at me now, and that is, 'But all my life through, the very insistence on truth has taught me the beauty of compromise.' Of late, I have had to learn the value of the words echoed again by Gandhi, 'Truth is hard as a diamond, and as tender as a blossom.'

My epiphany came now. My epiphany of negotiating this dichotomous man came after yet another sleepless night plowing through his writings, and recalling my chats with Uncle Hassim. My husband, finding me one morning exhausted, bedraggled and obviously having not slept a wink, spoke to me.

'I know you are struggling to understand Gandhi, and also reconcile what happened on the farms. And perhaps you have a point. He could not and did not, as one man, go to each and every hovel that the indentured farmers were living in.'

I reared my head to argue, but I held back. I thought about how Winnie Mandela, who was a firebrand by all standards, a vocal fighter against injustice in any way or form, had been gentle in her essay on Gandhi outlined in the huge volume that my Dad had gifted me. Winnie, whose dichotomy I had forgiven because I read her own words, spoke of Gandhi kindly. As a researcher and a critical thinker, I do not romanticise Gandhi, nor do I spend my time maligning him. I am a person in process, forming and then re-forming my own views on everything in my life. I know that amongst many South Africans, Gandhi is viewed as elitist, and perhaps he was. But I also know that his evolution did come.

Maybe all of this came late. Maybe the people on the farms, being whipped and often killed, finding suicide sometimes the best option, and those that never did escape it all and live with the scars in their genealogy today, could have known Gandhi better. He could have made himself accessible to these people by coming to see what really was happening on those farms. But again, he was one man, and he did what he could. He established the Phoenix settlement,* which is a distance away from the deep heart of the farms, and in this place he began to galvanise political consciousness in the people that stayed at his ashram.

I am reminded now of this drive to keep the Gandhian spirit alive in South Africa. Or perhaps it

---

*Gandhi established the Sarvodaya ashram and farm in Phoenix in then Zululand (now KwaZulu Natal) in 1904.

is to introduce the Gandhian spirit in the first place, because when I hit the ground and ask people of many backgrounds and ages how much they know of Gandhi, it is very little in the Indian community. Everyone can rote repeat what we all have read. But, truthfully, not many grew up speaking of him in terms of a Mahatma. This is probably where I fit into the frame of reference. The South African Indians have moved far away from the canefields now. They spend their time rejecting all aspects of having once been 'Coolies'. I think that in trying to keep the Gandhian spirit alive, it is these very descendants of Coolies that need to be accessed, told about the contrast within the mind of a man who they feel is so far above them that they don't reach out to even his ideals as a means to find comfort. Apartheid deleted him from our history books, but apartheid is over now. Young people need to be able to feel that they can reach out and touch Gandhi by his words.

The elitism was not by Gandhi himself. He may have started out that way, and evolved by his own admission into a fierce fighter for the vulnerable and poor. The elitism is the appropriation of Gandhi by people who keep him like a memento, and don't take him out of that 'manicured glass box' which I think he would have abhorred.

This year, 2018, marks 125 years since Gandhi was evicted from the first-class compartment of a train bound for the Transvaal. This event, many say, was his wake-up call into the appalling lives that Indian people had to survive under the apartheid regime. I tacitly assume that as a barrister trained in London, he might have heard whispers about apartheid and known a little of what racism it enforced. I know that the White South African government did not allow much news to leak out about whatever dirty linen was hiding in the closets, and if this dirty laundry did reach London or India, it may have been a watered-down version.

Nevertheless, as I spoke of earlier, this 125-year-old eviction and the parable-like birth of political consciousness in the barrister was celebrated in grand style with combined efforts by the Indian and South African governments, beginning on 2 October 2018 and continuing well beyond the Mahatma's birth anniversary, in an orchestrated publicity campaign of Gandhi Awareness. Banners, colour schemes and a surge of willing journalists who were suddenly spouting Gandhisms. As someone who sees the world in contrasts, meaning no shades of grey, I had to laugh out loud at one particular planned event. On 6 June 2018, both our governments held a swish dinner for politicians, dignitaries and celebrities. The next day, after this dinner that could have fed thousands instead of the three hundred famous guests, the invitees travelled on a train similar to the one Gandhi was evicted from. When the train arrived in Pietermaritzburg, a reenactment of the actual eviction took place using children from schools. I was not one of the invited celebrities, but I did follow the media frenzy that followed. On social media, politicians and pretty girls who had won the Miss India South Africa beauty pageant posed in the finest zardosi, embroidered chiffon salwars, sherwani suits and heavy Kanjivaram silk sarees, taking selfies inside the carriage decorated in not-easy-to-drape khadi cloth imported from India. In one picture, an elated politician turned man-about-town stands posing in a Modi-style waistcoat, his arm around a toothy socialite with large earrings. They actually do a pout selfie in front of a large sign saying #Satyagraha (Hashtag Satyagraha). Doordarshan and South African Broadcast Corporation reporters interview people on where they bought their outfits, whilst young Black girls carry around platters of pakoras and sushi. If there was anyone from a poor farmer or a council flat, who had entertained the thought of joining in the commemoration of Gandhi's tragic A-ha moment, I doubt this party would have attracted them to trying to get to know the Mahatma. Like a man I met in a shop where we were both feeling around for the best bhindi to buy, told me days after: 'Jaah (slang for yes). I saw it on TV. I wonder how much money they spent for the "lukka chow" (slang for tasty food). Maybe they should've given me the money to pay rent.'

It came to me in a flash then, what I have always been mulling over: Gandhi and his fights and his principles were lofty and great and achieved amazing things to uplift a people who were dying. But, here is my question—if he came here today, to modern-day South Africa, would only the rich be allowed to have an audience with him? Would anyone else even care?

In her book, *Gandhi's Prisoner? The Life of Gandhi's Son Manilal*, Gandhi's granddaughter, Uma Dhupelia-Mesthrie, echoes the words of her father Manilal's friend, the American Homer Jack as saying: 'The day will come when the name of Gandhi will be honoured in all South Africa as it is now in the world. No longer secretly remembered, the name of Gandhi will be openly honoured.'

As a collation of my own thoughts, and my conclusion to a very meandering written piece, I muse out loud whether this day has naturally come upon South Africa, or is it something that Gandhian scholars and the Gandhi family have been working tirelessly to reach. Have we begun engineering a relevance to Gandhi that serves popular politics now in a country that is scratching the dust for heroes? I think we have. Is it too late? The commemorations and the books and speeches still have not reached the sugarcane fields.

The watchtower in iMona—the one where the watcher sat looking for fires, would have been something Gandhi would have enjoyed seeing. Hearing children screaming 'Aag aati hai', would have resonated with him very much. Only, he never did see that watcher, or hear those children's voices. It was a double loss. Gandhi sadly lost out on the beautiful sight of actually seeing first-hand how some of the people of indenture were slowly growing in strength due to his work in raising their plight to government awareness, and many people, including young children, lost the chance to see, feel, touch and talk to the man who had done so much to abolish indenture.

The Safety of Silence
Why I Am An Activist

It is March 2017 and I am a grown woman, having a raging argument with my father. Like a petulant teenager, I shout at this man of almost seventy, 'You just don't get it, you just don't get me. You never have and you never will.'

I slam the car door, remembering the number of times I had raised my voice to say the same words to him over the years, and slammed bedroom doors in his face. But, his stubbornness runs in my veins too, and it seems the gaping maw between us has never healed. We have sustained a fragile circling of each other over the years, but some wounds can never be healed. Simply because they are too veiled in silence. Maybe I should just resign myself to the horrible fact that he will always disapprove of the choices I am now making. But, maybe, there is some hope in me that one day, the answers can be found. Until then, slammed doors and weeks of silence pervades our relationship.

I drive away from my childhood home on a sugarcane farm in rural KwaZulu Natal, a town called Tongaat, which draws its fame from being the home of the colonial Hulett Sugar Company, and one of the first places that began to grow sugarcane and mill sugar. My mouth is sour-tasting. In this town, where my father and his father were born, many people have never tasted sweetness. My childhood was blissfully sweet but as I have grown up I see now in retrospect that the older people that lived in the farm have suffered a great deal of bitter hardships.

In my rear-view mirror I can see him now, his thick old cardigan that he refuses to throw away, and that halo of grey hair, the colour makes me feel twinges of guilt as I see him turn around in his shuffling towelling slippers.

I drive through canefields. The rage sweeps through me on undulating stalks, bright green, moving like a sine wave. Memories will not fade. This latest argument will probably get shelved with all the others. Our arguments have always been about politics. Specifically, about my insistence on being involved in the politics of South Africa, and his almost terrified bullying of me to stay as far away from it as possible. Today, he raged at me for writing an opinion piece in a newspaper about the numerous civil marches that are razing through our country.

A week ago, the President of the African National Congress, and the President of South Africa, Jacob Zuma, fired our finance minister, Pravin Gordhan, in an unexpected cabinet reshuffle that saw the nation gape in horror as we immediately were downgraded to junk status, and the nation feared for the looming threat of State Capture by a group of businessmen from India. A band of brothers who seemingly had the President's ear and filled his pockets. Pravin Gordhan had been protecting the state coffers from corrupt business dealings and looting, and now he was fired. The country went into a state of mayhem. Marches were organised across the land, and I was determined to join the people in raising my fist in the air and marching, writing about it and exposing my politics on the frontline. My father was deeply distressed. He regarded my opinion piece with distaste. Or was it fear? He forbade me to march. I ignored him. I was not a teenager anymore.

***

I still recall the moment when I became politically aware. It was the mid-80s, and I was thirteen years old, attending a sporting event. Apartheid was at its peak, riots and arrests were the common order. My best friend's brother was being watched by the Apartheid Special Branch for being an inciter against the White Apartheid Rule. At this sports event, I recall the loudspeakers suddenly squealing and we all blocked our ears. The announcements about long jump and relays stopped abruptly and we saw a scuffle in the announcer's tent. A group of boys, probably all in high school and early university, had grabbed the microphone and began playing Pink Floyd's *Brick in the Wall*. Then the voice of my friend's brother came booming out, loud and clear.

'Free Mandela. End Apartheid!'

His words spread like a chant. I felt my entire body react, I jumped up with the rest of the teenagers in the crowd, and hundreds of us took up the chant. I will never forget the power I felt in that moment, the strains of Roger Water's lyrics being modified to 'We don't need no White Apartheid.'

My friend's brother was arrested that day. No one, not even her, spoke of him after that. Such was the silence of my small town. He was just a stupid rebel. Stupid for raising his voice.

But I became obsessed. In the absence of all political literature, which was banned, and radio and television only showing us Afrikaans-dubbed versions of *Little House on the Prairie*, I secretly began to meet with a group of high school and university students behind the old Town Library. We discussed, we debated, and we became inflamed with all the knowledge of the facts we were denied. Taking home little pamphlets called 'Frank Talk' written by the late Steve Biko, and even braving some Communist literature distributed by the banned ANC, I would hide them inside fashion magazines or Archie comics. My parents suspected nothing. Our group began to plan a large school boycott in solidarity with the countrywide marches and boycotts to free Nelson Mandela, who was then known as a dangerous terrorist. The boycott was to be our swansong. If the police took us, then so be it.

My father found out about what I had been doing the day before the planned boycott, and swept through the house like a simoom, removing all my precious literature and ordering my mother to burn the pamphlets near the old water tap. Burn them till they were ashes, and then wash the ashes down the drain. I ran through the house, screaming my head off, grabbing at pages from his arms, but coming up with just torn fragments of words that had fuelled my secret nightly reading. Everything was burned. And now that I had been found out, not by any Apartheid Special Branch Police, but by my own father, he pieced a jigsaw puzzle together and forbade me to go to the march the next day. I was tearful, furious, betrayed by my own father. Couldn't he see that this was the most alive I had ever felt, that this was my moment, my time to fight for my freedom and my future? He could see none of it. He just locked me in my room till the day was over. I missed the boycott, and my heart was broken.

I didn't let up easily, and neither did he. Our relationship was broken by that moment. He began to watch everything I did, insisting I read the poems of John Donne or Shakespeare's plays instead. I recall him making me stand and recite English poetry by rote at the dinner table. And when I blandly went through my performance of 'to see the world in a grain of sand,' with all the passion of a dish-rag, he would calm down. These are the words of our oppressors, our colonial masters, I would shout at him at the end, and stalk away, leaving my young siblings tense and upset. My mother was always silent.

I relented. For peace, as I prepared to finish high school and enter university, I simply gave in. I learnt to play lawn tennis and to sit with my ankles neatly crossed while discussing the latest episode of *Knight Rider*, that mechanical voice of the talking car dubbed into incongruous Afrikaans.

'Good,' my father said, watching my reticence. 'Good. We must always be quiet, because it is safer that way.' I hated his reticence with bitter gall.

* * *

I was in my first year of university when Nelson Mandela was released. One of the first towns he decided to visit was my home-town. A huge red-carpet event was planned for Mandela, where he was to be given the Key to the Town. Just a few years ago, most people in this town thought him a terrorist. I was insistent on going. My father kept an inexpungible silence. I was to be married that same year. What would people say? That his daughter focused less on cooking skills and more on politics? He forbade me.

It was my mother who finally broke her silence. She defied him, and agreed to take me to the Town

Hall. Both of us were moved to tears as this tall, beautiful man spoke with such dignity and grace, and thanked the Tongaat family that had hid him under the guise of a petrol attendant at their gas station. He enveloped the old sari-clad mother of the family in a huge bear hug, saying that it was her tasty curries that fortified him in those dark days when he hid in tin shacks near our farm.

But, for me it was not only Nelson Mandela's presence that made my heart squeeze into an emotional ball. It was the look on my mother's face. She looked like a woman whose butterfly wings were opening wide and strong. I asked her about it afterwards. She approached sensitive topics that had been hidden for years in her way of explanation.

My mother told me of how my great grandfather had come to South Africa from India as an indentured labourer with nothing to his name but a promise of a new life. He had laboured and struggled in dangerous conditions but had never been able to buy his passage back to India because of a fraudulent document called a 'girmit'.

Strange name, I muttered to her.

'Well, the document that promised Indians a free passage back to the motherland, India, was called an agreement, which almost all of them could not read. Simply placing their thumbprint on it made it a watertight if not sinister deal. They later learned that the document had many small print clauses, and they would never be able to gain their free passage back to India after paying innumerable taxes, fines and penalties heaped upon them for things as ridiculous as singing out loud in the fields. In distaste and rage they cursed this agreement, and slowly the word morphed into their own heady mix of Bhojpuri, Hindi, Tamil and the local African language, Zulu, into a swear word...Girmit. This word then became a title for those that laboured in the fields. They were called "Girmitiyas".'

My mother knew all this, despite the fact that she did not descend from indentured labourers, and her grandfather had arrived in South Africa with more to his name than the ability to wield a sickle. But she had spent long hours talking to her father-in-law, my Dadaji, and learned the history of his tragic lineage.

His father, having learned that he would never be able to return to his beloved village of Gorakhpur in Uttar Pradesh, did what any man with a family could do. He made this land, South Africa his home, although it never did feel like home to anyone.

Slowly, he began to build a tiny world for his progeny. None of his children, including my grandfather, were educated or literate. They were just labourers.

My grandfather's name was Dhunpath. He showed great resourcefulness and an ability to make money. Perhaps names do follow their owners after all. He refused to be a simple farm labourer or a sugar mill worker. He had big dreams, and in his dreams only one word echoed...land.

He had taught himself the art of building, and soon became sought after to build some of Tongaat's most well-known buildings. They still stand today. But no one would know that an illiterate farmer had designed and built them. Despite this explanation, I still did not understand my father's vehemence against my political involvements. I argued, and my mother told me to be patient and listen.

'Your father was ten years old, and he had found a tattered copy of a novel at one of the construction sites that he would tag along to. One day, waiting for your grandfather to finish his work, Daddy was sitting on the floor reading this book, when suddenly a Special Branch policeman grabbed him by the ear and tore the book from him. The book was called *Black Beauty* by Anna Sewell, a book about a sleek black horse and nothing else.

'The policeman began to beat your Daddy for reading a book that it was rumoured the apartheid President Verwoed had banned in South Africa because he believed the words Black and Beauty did not belong together, and that it would incite Black people into feeling superior. Your Dada came running to where his son was being beaten and begged the policeman to beat him instead of the child. The policeman turned on Dada, and although Dada was a strong, tall man who had been brought up on hard labour, he curled up into a ball, allowing the young White policeman to demean and beat him. The greatest injuries your Dada sustained were the humiliation of seeing his young son watch him get beaten without daring to fight back, repeating "Sorry Baas (Boss in Afrikaans), sorry Baas" repeatedly.'

My mother ended her tale. We were sitting in the car outside the Town Hall, the lavish function now over. She looked at me and she had tears in her eyes.

'Do you know the fear we had for the Apartheid Police? You will never know. My brother was almost jailed because he had kept a few pamphlets of ANC literature in our house, and we had to race through the house at midnight and hide them when we heard the Special Branch was coming. Your father is not

cruel, nor is he ignorant of politics. He is simply
afraid of losing you. He could see you had this fire
in you from a young age and he was afraid for you.
Now do you understand?'

I did understand better. But I knew that Mandela
had been released and there were no longer threats
from the Apartheid Police. But, sadly, threats to
any women in politics and those who were openly
vocal about any injustice, came anyway, subversively.
Society did not look well upon women and girls,
especially from the Indian diaspora who became
politicised or sociologically critical. I ended up
marrying, forgetting my dreams of studying political
science, and settling into domesticity. Many years
later, I did enter university, older than the eighteen-
year-olds who carried books clutched to their chests
and had no interest in the subject other than its
pass-mark at examinations. I gained a degree, I
wrote articles, and now I write books. My father
still fears for me, this girl-woman writing such
inciteful, dangerous words. At first I thought he
was a chauvinist and did not approve of a woman
who stepped out of that confined world of kitchen-
bedroom-kitchen. But now I realise he is far from
being a chauvinist. He is a father to a girl who

refuses to be quiet, and with that comes deep fear
only a parent will know. He comes from a lineage
of people who were lashed and killed for speaking
out. It is no wonder he has settled into silence.

Although I know now about my father's fears, our
relationship has not healed. I am now a parent too,
of children who will grow up as South Africans of
Indian descent. This too is a nebulous and frightening
world that they will have to inhabit. They will have
to forge an identity out of nothing much, but a
mixed-up idea of who and what they are. I am a
mother of both a boy and a girl. Often I wonder
what I will do if either of them decide to enter into
social and political worlds. Will it be better if my son
decides to become politically active, rather than my
daughter? Do I persist in teaching them Urdu and
Gujarati (our home languages), knowing that they
will only ever speak those languages behind doors
and curtains, and will be judged for not learning
African languages? Will they one day endure a
beating because they admired a book? These will
be worlds that I can never reach down and save
them from. My answers are never clear enough to
convince me that I would do otherwise from what
my father did to me. South Africa currently is in a

place where civil action hearkens back to the days
of rebellion before apartheid was banned. Now,
should either of my children, boy or girl, decide to
fight injustice, the fight will be equally dangerous.
As a mother, I will fear for them, just as my father
feared for me. But, I won't stop them. Nor will I
ever stop myself. This crevasse between my father
and me asks for healing.

I want to turn my car around and head back to
my parents' home, that farmhouse with its beautiful
inner courtyard where the women used to dry bright
red chillies on the lids of huge pots. My world is still
stuck in the frieze of a farmhouse built by hand by
my grandfather and his seven sons. I know that I
will find my father on the latticed veranda with his
glasses perched on his nose, reading the newspaper.
I hope he is reading my article.

Shades of Brown and Black
The New Apartheid Is Money

The Archbishop Desmond Tutu, an iconic South African freedom fighter and one of the most candid truth tellers in my country, coined the term 'Rainbow Nation' for South African society post-apartheid. In this term, his aim was to encompass and unify every colour of person under the African sun, and foster a moniker of unity in a country that had only seen inequality based on skin colour. As it played out in the many years since the abolition of apartheid, we all learned basic physics—when you unify all the colours, they become the colour Black, and in this nebulous process, there are different shades of Black. Let me explain.

After Nelson Mandela took his long walk to freedom from the gates of Robben Island, there came an influx of unification strategies, that the

African National Congress at the time realised was necessary to prevent a civil war. The academic and studied manner of Nelson Mandela translated into beautiful photo-ops for the world to see, but in reality his work had only just begun. It was 1994, and I was just entering into political awareness (albeit secretly). My secrecy was based on the fear of my own parents, who had their own preconceived fear of the danger of politics in South Africa, as was the case with most parents at the time. What was highly evident was that many of these parents were of Indian origin. Much like the immigrant ethos the world over, the tendency was to keep your head down, be silent, work hard and keep away from the limelight as much as possible. This ethos, a survival guide to being neither Black nor White, served to allow many of us to slip through the system in silence, and move through a country as if this country was just a temporary housing space. Many people of my generation inhabited this island of facelessness with ease. Many did not. Now, in current South Africa in 2018, it is the ones who did not go silently along who have a great deal of animosity towards the ones that did.

Those of us Indians who were born in South

Africa owned our citizenship as South Africans, and not citizens of India. Although we had a cultural and linguistic tie to being Indian, we were South African citizens, many of whom had struggled during apartheid and had fought the subjugation of people of colour. We thought of ourselves as Black, we called ourselves Black. Many of our community annoyed us greatly by using the term 'us Indians'.

But, from 1994 to 2018 is a long time. This time saw the one thing that was a game-changer, and that was economics. Equality morphed into equity, and there was no denying that under the apartheid regime, Indian South Africans had amassed much more equity than Black South Africans. The atrocious living conditions of Black South Africans, their lack of access to fundamental human needs like shelter, clean water, sanitation, employment and education was vastly different to Indian South Africans.

Before the abolition of apartheid, the White regime created a system that clearly divided before it could unify. The winds of change had been blowing in parliament for a long while, the savvy politicians knowing that change was going to come long before they publicly gave into it. In the 1980s, the government began to sow seeds of discord by creating a system called the Tricameral System, a term that brings up the gall of many activists. The reason being, this system served to eradicate all the efforts of the freedom fighters who were Indian and Coloured (mixed race—an accepted South African term for the population group—*see Preface*). The Tricameral System, as its name suggests, gave the vote to three population groups. The House of Assembly was for White South Africans. The House of Representatives was for Coloured South Africans, and the House of Delegates was for Indian South Africans. This malicious system now set people against each other. Rights to education and basic human needs such as housing was given by the White regime to Indians and Coloureds. And the Blacks were lumped into a very separate unit called by the derogatory name 'Bantu Affairs'. The use of the word Bantu itself arouses the ire of many. It is tantamount to using the N-word in America. It goes without saying that the Blacks did not have the right to vote, until South Africa's first democratic election in 1994, following the release of Nelson Mandela, when the African National Congress was recognised as a political party.

The truth is that people of Indian descent were less oppressed than the Blacks during apartheid. They were sent to live in townships such as Chatsworth or Phoenix, but the delivery of basic services such as sanitation and electricity to these townships was significantly better than that of Black townships such as Soweto or Umlazi. South African Indians also had better access to education and the schools were in significantly better condition.

There were many South African Indian people who lapped up all that was on offer, joined the House of Delegates, and pandered to their new master who had thrown them the bone. This particular system saw South African Indians prosper economically under the apartheid regime. Whilst many Indian activists rallied vehemently to boycott the House of 'Dele-goats' as we called it, the majority went the safe route, and accepted the benefits without a qualm. And that worked to the relative advantage of Indians, an advantage that still exists today. An advantage that has created animosity between Black South Africans towards Indian South Africans.

***

Following the abolition of apartheid, one of the systems that was put in place by the African National

Congress was Black Economic Empowerment. Here, in an act of levelling the economic playing fields, Black South Africans were given access to mandatory inclusion in companies, universities and programmes in quota systems. Under this system, Indians were now considered Black. This 'regrouping' gave them the advantage of being included in the economic structures of benefit meant for the Blacks, and many having come from positions of advantage anyway— like being passenger Indians and not labourers that came from India—and having embraced the Tricameral System benefits, their advantage again saw them placed higher than Black South Africans. Leading economists have debated this since 1994. Most have argued there were no grounds for making Indians beneficiaries of Black Economic Empowerment policies.

Even though we were all oppressed, we were not equally oppressed. The result of this inequality again began sowing seeds of anger that Black South Africans feel towards Indian South Africans.

I do not doubt that post 1994, the Indian population was more advantaged. I see it in my own friends and family. Many of my cousins are medical doctors who were given places in leading medical colleges during the apartheid regime. I look around me and see that the majority of Indian South Africans live in homes that far surpass the squatter camp shacks that Black South Africans still live in. Every single person I know of Indian descent has a domestic helper, including myself. And the domestic help, the maid and the gardener—they are always Black. I once spoke to a beggar at a traffic light, a young able-bodied SA Indian woman, and I asked that instead of me handing money to her, would she consider coming to my house to do some ironing on a regular basis to earn her money. She laughed and told me she would rather beg than do domestic work. Yet, my Black African domestic helper, Sindisiwe, willingly does this work rather than begging. She lives in a shack in a squatter camp. Her children live hundreds of kilometres away in the Eastern Cape. She sees them twice a year, at Easter and at Christmas. I suffer from guilt every time I hand her a pile of clothes to launder. In the spectrum of this rainbow nation, there are different shades of dark. This raises a very dichotomous space in my mind. I know that in providing Sindisiwe with a job, which due to her previous racial disadvantage she does not have the basic education to secure, I am empowering her and her children whose school fees I pay for. But, I also am reliant on her labours as a domestic worker who does the things for me that I am too busy, and too inept to do.

Another example of this class divide that still exists today is transport. If I need to go anywhere, from the supermarket to a dinner date, I am able to immediately climb in my car and drive there. As I drive to my destination, around me there are many mini-bus taxis (a common sight in South Africa, where a mini-van is used as a cheap means of transporting people), and this form of transport is mainly used by the Black people. I drive past the universities and colleges and see lines of Black students waiting at dusk for their mini-bus taxi to take them back home after a long day in college, and I know this home will probably be a low-income flat, shared residence or even a squatter camp in an informal settlement. I also see young Indian, White and a sprinkling of Black or Coloured students driving through the university gates in fancy cars, with loud music blaring. No one can tell me that such a daily occurrence does not display a class or economic divide on display in the new South Africa.

Not all SA Indians live with this privilege. I have

noticed a small change in that in these mini-bus taxis (which for me have become a sort of symbol for the inequities between people), there are some Indian faces that stare blankly out of the windows as dusk draws in. I once saw a White boy take a mini-bus taxi, and I was not the only person staring at him in disbelief. But, there is no doubt that if transportation was a snapshot of the inequity in South Africa, this snapshot will show that Black people are still at the bottom of the privilege heap.

During apartheid, Indians were subjugated by the White regime, but were still considered superior to Coloured and Black people. Although the state of things has supposedly changed, this mindset still exists in SA Indian communities today. The truth is that many SA Indian people still do not accept Black South Africans as equals, and the parallel result of this is that there are instances of hate speech and racial slurs that are meted out in both directions. SA Indians who feel that the Blacks are now benefiting too much from Black Economic Empowerment and Affirmative Action become bitter and angry, as they watch their children lose places at universities in quota systems, or not get jobs despite qualifications. Blacks, on the other hand, look at SA Indians living in relatively better homes and driving good cars, eating out at shopping malls and wearing expensive clothes, and begin to believe that all SA Indians benefited from apartheid.

It seems that once apartheid was abolished, a new line of separation has been drawn. Money. The divide now is between the haves and the have-nots, and skin colour does not enter the party. I have known people of all races and colour who are firm friends and business associates simply by virtue of the Lamborghinis and Benzs parked in their garages, the fine private schools all their kids go to in an Old Boys' Club-type situation, and the expensive holidays they go on together three times a year. Contrarily, I know people of all races, including White people, who live in low-income flats, struggling with the municipality for garbage collection and sending their children together to the same overcrowded public schools.

The shades of brown and black in contemporary South Africa are now melding together into people who struggle. And the new Struggle is not colour, it is survival.

Canefields

And the Winner is..

Supper time at the Dala household, and a full-on war is afoot!

The bones of contention this time are not the ones in the proverbial Wednesday night gravy and potatoes. Larger issues are at stake here. And the standard head on a plate is: Identity. Large pickings for a six-year-old boy, a nine-year-old girl, an overgrown teenager called husband, and two sixty-something grandparents. But before I even go there, let me explain.

You don't know me, but I suppose from the fruit salad that is my name, you might have surmised some oddities. I hail from a mix of Hindu indentured labourer stock who went on to become farmers, from my father's side, and, maternally, Muslim artisan and trader stock who were not indentured, but were free ning their own businesses. Their tales of begin in a village in India, continue on a crossing the Kala Pani (they called it the dark waters), finally to land on the East Coast of Africa. My father listens into this identity war being played out, and reminds me that the title of the diary he has kept of his Bihari mother's storytelling still bears the name of the cow that caused this migration. In fact, I joke, the cow's name was probably Kala. She was a black cow with a betel-leaf shaped white distinguishing mark on her forehead, my father tells me. 'Well, Babu, why am I not surprised?' I say playfully. 'A Black and White cow, not any shade of brown. How typical.'

My father rebukes me, growing serious and ruminative. This cow holds special significance in my father's legacy. In the story that is told to us, my great-grandfather, suffering grossly from middle-child syndrome in his village near Gorakhpur, Uttar Pradesh, became incensed when his favourite cow was sold off. Feeling largely victimised, he decided to run away, and in his rebellious sojourn away from his home, he happened upon a Sirdar, a recruiter from the East India Company, who offered him a chance to work and live in a land that was paved

with gold. His anger and rebellion made him follow
bands of such men, in search of a life that would
magically transform them from farmyard minions
to Brahmins and overbearing patriarchs.

Now, I have an aunt, older than my father, named
Parvathie, who everyone just calls Bhoujie in pure
Bhojpuri style. She tells me a different tale. She
ignores the seventeen-year-old boy who petulantly
threw a tantrum over a cow, and talks about my
great grandmother. Her tale is somewhat more
romantic, and I feel intrinsically inclined to adopt
this tale. Bhoujie always has been a source of the
most accurate and authentic information thus far,
and in this quest, I am not going to doubt her now.

She talks of my great-grandmother who grew
up in a village near Patna in Bihar. Her name was
Bhagirathee, and well...she ran away. I almost choke
with laughter each time I think of Bhagirathee who
did 'bhag'.

Something academic in me ticks against my skull
saying that maybe her name was something else, but
because she ran away, she defiantly chose this name.
I may be stretching my inner Rigoberta Menchu a
little too far on that one. Nevertheless, it is stated
in her ship records that she was twenty-eight and

of the Noniya caste. I have no idea what a Noniya caste is, but I know that when we were growing up my girl cousins would get slightly bitchy when they saw a girl with untied hair, jhumka earrings and clad in very bright colours, dancing on a stage to singer Kanchan's song, 'Chadar bichao balma.'

'Dekh! Besharam Noniya,' they would say. Spit sideways. Eye roll.

Shall I tell them now, in their mansions and their beige, that they descended from a Besharam Noniya?

And the layers form and form over and over again in my life where I am laughed at by my children's father when I attempt dancing to the Kanchan song. He calls it low caste music. My father stops expounding in Bhojpuri. The identity game has now introduced a sensitive word. Caste...

'Many villagers from India ran away to escape the caste system,' I tell my allegedly high-caste Mullah-named husband. He struggles to understand even my tone.

The caste system is not practised at all in South Africa as an open means of identification. We have all just melded into a cauldron. But it used to be rampant when the ships arrived in the 1800s.

In their book, *Inside Indenture: A South African*

Story, 1860–1914, Ashwin Desai and Goolam Vahed quote the White editor of the *Natal Mercury's* description of the arrival of the first 'batch' of Indians in the paper's edition on 22 November 1860. The editor, one John Robinson, describes the wild and flashing eyes of the few women on the ship with long dishevelled hair and well-formed figures; and men with scraggy 'Oriental' skin and inquisitive glances. Often, I take Ashwin and Goolam's book out of my bookcase late at night, not having anyone to converse with because everyone I know wants to forget and erase their lineage. And when I hold their beautiful book on my knees, finger pointing at names that just clutch at me, Ramdeen and Meenatchi, just for the sake of touching their names, I recall that back then class and caste dissolved in the briny Indian Ocean. Now in South Africa, when the fate of the Indians is so tremulous, when we are being accused of benefiting from colonialism and apartheid and told that Africa belongs to Africans, the spirit of the jahaji of no caste is gone. The jahajis formed a strong brotherhood on board the ships in the 1800s, brothers who despite religion and skin colour and caste bonded together to simply survive in the new dominion to which they were being sent. It is now that dominion that is being fought over, and somehow casteism is entering the equation much like the jahajibhais forgot each other after they descended from the shiphold and stepped onto the plank of opportunity.

An all-pervasive characteristic of the migration from India was that once on board the ship out of Calcutta or Madras, caste meant nothing to the Englishman. It didn't matter how much a Brahmin whined or shouted. He had to lie on a dirty blanket next to a Dalit, and of course, eat the salted fish and dhall chaval with stones meant for them all. It is noted in exhaustively interesting texts by writer colleagues of mine that very few Brahmin caste people were actually recruited, as they were seen to have hands that were too soft, and a body not made for labour.

But, arriving in Durban, as they formed higgledy-piggledy lines to get their official passes and identification documents, suddenly almost everyone was claiming to be of Brahmin or Kshatriya caste. They came with last names like Balram and Gareeb, but suddenly in their documents, this surname, Maharaj, arose. And with it came a deluge of Singhs who were by all appearance farm labourers from

Bihar but now claimed a Sikh leaning to their lineage. Anyway, what did the Englishman know? Suckled on the teats of colonialism from birth, he rolled his eyes at the natives and wrote down the easy-to-spell names. Maharaj. Singh. Forget the nomenclature of the long-winded Bhanwarielalls and Dwarikapersads. But I digress.

My dearest source of information, Bhoujie, tells a tale of a young woman in Bihar, fierce and headstrong, who ran away from her husband and possibly, young children, because she saw a chance of a better life. Bhoujie would always eye me in her sideways glance, and often say to my father, 'that one is like...That One.' My father gracefully ignores her. But he knows.

* * *

The dinner table story that began this diatribe, is unfolding in heated discussions now. The dessert is served, hot sooji halwa. My mother looks at my husband and they both grin. In his culture (Gujarati Muslim), the dessert is served before the main meal. But my mother, whose father came from India not as a labourer but a passenger Indian, has learnt to sweeten the mouth later than sooner. Now, the complexity unfolds where I am a heady mix of a Hindu Bihari runaway wild-woman and a hot-headed UP cowherd (paternal), and a moneyed passenger Indian literate in Urdu, Hindi and the arts (maternal). My father is a farm labourer turned schoolteacher, my mother is a pampered tennis club daughter.

In the writing of my own history, I have in a matter of choice and of circumstance ended up siding with the labourer side of my lineage. Darker-skinned, down and out though they were, planting dhania and sugarcane, I just could not bring myself to enjoy the white tennis skirt, silk salwar family gatherings of the other side, the passenger Indian side. Maybe it just feels more revolutionary to side with the underdog. But believe me, underdogs they never were. They were fighters, and in just three or four generations went from being lower caste Bihari people in a ship's bowels to producing great academics, doctors, lawyers, businessmen and one errant writer.

My husband, on the other hand, is of only second-generation Surti Muslim trader lineage. This means, as he puts it, he is a 'pure-bred' Mullah caste Muslim with businesses and properties in Surat, Gujarat.

His grandfathers on both maternal and paternal sides arrived here in *Portus Natalus* with money in their pockets and I am strangely aware that inside the shiphold, my ancestor probably didn't even have pockets. Or trousers. An awfully weather-beaten dhoti perhaps.

Now this particular mix-up elicits strange reactions from all interested parties, notwithstanding that should we have married in the 60s, we might have escaped the atrocious South African Immorality Act which punished inter-racial marriages with arrest, but we would certainly have been victims of a secular act of some sort that might have seen us flee to some nebulous, non-denominational island of all acceptance. We were lucky. Compromises were made. His pure Mullah breed took the sting, and began loving the mixed-name girl well enough.

But the battle for identity has begun closing ranks as it tends to do when the honeymoon is over, and the babies are born. And this brand new identity search now belongs to the offspring. We both want dominion.

My husband advances his attack by regaling the confused little things with story upon story about his growing up days in Town. I have to admit, I am entranced. Town! The great big city of Durban, where jazz clubs, ballroom dancing and fashionable clothes could be bought. But dare you stick your grotty non-White nose onto the pure white storefront of Garlicks, and salivate over fish paste and brown sauce, you'd get a few hard raps on your head with a baton. No matter your breeding and heritage. Brown and black noses were sharply disjointed. Still, in my growing up years, although we were never allowed to use the staircases, benches, beaches or streets labelled 'Whites Only', Durban Town held a fascination for me. In my case it was only a little to do with the sexy dances and tucked away nightclubs. It was more that Durban was the heart of where the anti-apartheid revolutionaries went to shout their speeches at a platform called Red Square, and to march boldly with fists in the air. I wanted that more than I wanted a jazz dance with a handsome Town boy. Now that I have my posh handsome Town boy, the pendulum swings against my wishes, and I yearn for the simplicity of running with a familiarly handsome farm boy through the loamy earth of a sugarcane field. I think that parts of me dream romance in Bhojpuri, whilst parts of me dream it in Urdu. I've accepted my dichotomy, and my husband's Gujarati consolations miss the mark.

He is proud of his Town. He shows it off like a prize in every conversation, much like I wield the crown of my sugarcane field. He talks about running away from Anjuman Islamic School and sneaking into the Shiraz or Avalon cinemas to watch angry young Amitabh battle his Gabbar. Playing cricket in the lane next to Afzal Building and the choice abuse of Gori Apa, whose precious chrysanthemums get knocked off their perch. Skulking around the dangers of the frustrating labyrinth of alleys that most call the Casbah, while others just go "Bah, humbug. It's just Durban, not Istanbul for goodness sakes".'

I picture a gang of naughty boys of various colours, some in white crocheted skull caps, some in fez caps, standing outside sari shops looking for the garachs (South African Gujarati slang for people who are easily conned by streetwise businessmen).

Well, here we are. Here come the garachs. From the plantations, ready to part with grubby money tied into handkerchiefs and tucked into bosoms in pouches.

Stiff and starchy in our crinoline lace dresses, taken out of almirahs just for this one trip, fresh from the farm, our once-yearly foray into the glitzy Town has us panting up a storm. Fringes too thick for comfort, and clunky shoes, we are paraded by our fathers into Studio Sydney for our annual family photograph.

Town, to us farmers, is tantamount to Hollywood. Handsome men and starlets on every corner. The reality being far removed, it was and still is a dangerous place. Still, on every corner, stand handsome men selling us garachs fake watches and 'real leather belts'. We buy them. They give us a taste of this nectar. Town.

A frustrated father waits patiently outside Shrimati's Saree boutique, and gives into the spiel of the Fountain Lane raconteur with coiffed, pomaded hair, who sells him a transistor radio. Our starchy petticoats in the world of Mary Quant have us bristling, the coconut oil dripping perhaps too close to home. Our egos are soothed with a spicy lunch at the Victory Lounge Cafe. We act like the rustics we are and plaster our faces against the window at Garlicks and receive a rap from the stick of a man who is whiter than anyone we have ever seen on the farm. The whitest person we know is a ruddy sugar baron named Colin, whom we've only seen from afar, on the back of his horse called Dickens.

But the Grey Street and Victoria Street Boys know

enough to laugh confidently at the White face and swagger away. Or perhaps they are laughing at us. How relieved we feel when we buy our laces from Eve's Elegance, pack our sarees and 'Town purchases' (plus fake transistor radio) into the old Valiant and make our long, long way back to the farm. Town is scary. Those alleyways, those hangers-on, those sights and sounds of cinemas and ice-cream parlours are not for us. We know. We still want a little bit of it anyway.

But, lest a Town boy stray his way into our home ground one day, how we relish the turn of the table. He arrives in his cream Moustache Suit, John Travolta in his high-heeled, gold-tipped footwear, and trips on sugarcane roots, and we know. He won't last a day. The threat of black mambas that never come, chicken curry from a fresh running kill, and his first view of a sky full of stars, and the next day the young lad is back on the bus. To Town. Back to his overpopulated claustrophobic Casbah.

* * *

I bring you back now to the war between the indentured labourer's child and the trader's child, both of whom want dominion over their combined progeny. Me, ever the researcher, suggests that we put this to the test. Who are these children really? Will they accept a lineage of the burned brown backs of bony men planting sugarcane, shouting 'Har har Mahadev' with each swing of the hoe, or will they lean towards the soft hands of women hidden behind lattice, writing Gujarati letters laced with duas to relatives in universities in Lahore?

I have to know. I will not rest. I suppose it doesn't escape me that while my ancestor was still trying to work out how to use a sickle without lopping his head off, my husband's ancestor was learning the subtleties of elaichie in the perfect biryani. Strange dichotomy that.

So, the experiment began with Saturday finding this mix-up of a family striding down Grey Street, into Victoria Street, snaking into Madressah Arcade and Kismet Arcade, dodging a million bodies at Victoria Street Market and peeping into the largest mosque in the southern hemisphere. Brave people, us. I certainly did not see glitz and glamour. I did see a few old stalwarts in tiny shops fixing clocks and selling bespoke buttons though. My husband used the time to stand and mutter with misty eyes about Jhavery's shoe shop and Shiraz who worked in Shiraz Arcade. Goofy's name came up a few times. That got the children smiling. A cat burglar called Luqman was mentioned, some googlies that Amra bowled in Victor Lane, and the swinging hips of Saadiya (Sadie), as she sauntered into the Goodwill Lounge. I had to pry him off the pavement, and bribe him with a hot dog from Tasty Eats to stop him from sobbing in nostalgia.

His Town had become nothing of what he remembered. Save for a few diehards, the entire City Centre had become ramshackle housing and shops selling African clothing, beads and traditional medicines made from bitter aloes. Meat roasted on hot coals right alongside butcheries, a snazzy name, Shisha Nyama (hot meat) given to these places where you got your meat and ate it too. Department stores dotted almost every building shopfront, and the word Garlicks had been madly painted over. The days of the corner grocer were dead. Now everyone could walk into Woolworths to buy shrink-wrapped mangoes, and no batons were wielded.

Like links in a chain, small but significant, were innumerable Chinese shops, selling everything from blankets to high fashion wedding dresses, and

Pakistani immigrant eateries brandishing bright red chicken tikka pieces on metal skewers. Zimbabwean and Nigerian traders sold peplum dresses, Bangladeshi traders sold bangles. The old trader Indians had fled the chaos, opting to settle and trade in expensive malls and shrub-lined suburbs instead.

Well, looking at my hot and bothered children as they watched the circus that is now Town, I high-fived the air. Surely, the Canefields would win now.

I was wrong. Sunday saw us dragging the tykes on an hour's drive into the sugarcane fields, rivers and mud of my youth. They were not impressed when I had my misty-eyed moments, describing the way we would net shrimp in the river using a potato sack and neem sticks, and run barefoot through a fullblown sugarcane fire. Showing them the first school I attended elicited guffaws. It had a huge water tank, and three classrooms. I was losing the war. My nine-year-old asked if this place had Wi-fi and I found myself cursing yet another type of Pad in my lifetime. My descriptive demonstrations of the coal stoves, the lanterns, the boreholes and the stinky dam were in vain. But I felt at peace. My husband hunted for garachs. My kids screamed their exit.

On the homeward journey from the sugarcane

farm to suburbia, which is a place neither my husband nor I have grown up in, I realised that all this history will never really matter to our children. Unless we constantly push them to see these places, to read our stories, to meet the old men and women who still hold these places and history dear in their hearts. All will be lost to a Stadium that began life as a basket but transmogrified into a swinging *Circ du Soleil* where young Indian children would rather listen to hip-hop and skateboard with their underwear showing.

Mention India and all you would get from our youth of Indian descent here is a description of Katrina Kaif's curves or whether *KKKG* or *DDLJ* or *KKHH* or *ADHM* is KJo's best work. I once asked a young niece if she had heard of Humayun or that King Ashoka was from Bihar. She retorted, 'Do they also act with Shraddha Kapoor?'

Suketu Mehta, in his magnificent novel, *Maximum City*, describes the Bombay of his birth through the eyes of his child who was born and grew up in New York. He returns to New Mumbai, and laments that his son will never know the pleasures of walking into a neighbour's flat unannounced for a hefty dinner, and a cuddle from everyone's grandma.

In a linguistic moment of nostalgia, he stands on a street in Manhattan and actually yearns to swear out loud in Hindi.

Yes, 'tis true indeed. It is Town, or perhaps you have a penchant for calling it Casbah. And yes, those were dirty, filthy canefields by all standards. People suffered deeply in both places. What matters is that our children will one day look at the ghosts of these places. We will no longer be there to tell them the stories.

I have made peace with lines and crossings, with mixed lineages and languages. I have made peace too with colourism and racism. What I have never made peace with yet is the silence of it all. The forgetting. The Erasure. Who cares if my children are a confused bundle of cane-cutter, shop owner, tinker, tailor, soldier, spy? I just care that they know that their history is a story that existed. And I will be that mother who tells them about it. Every day.

Of Bridal Veils and Monikers

My mother used to dress brides on the weekends. During the week, she was a teacher in a farm school, trying to paint the black chalkboard with colours of ABC when all the chalk they were given was just white. On the weekends, some sort of electric creativity would come alive in her, and she would gladly awake early and rush from farmhouse to farmhouse in our village, for certainly there was always a bride to dress.

I suppose now that I think about it, she had no particular skill in dressing brides, no special training in make-up artistry or draping. But, in our sugarcane farm village, my mother was fashionable. She had arrived as the daughter-in-law from the Big City. She had married my father in a love marriage, had thrown away all the fineries a life in the 'Town' of Durban offered her, including the many freedoms she had grown up with. Settling into farm life, with no running water, outdoor ablutions, coal stoves and oil lamps probably was not easy for her, especially since she had an education as a teacher, but I would never know the silent petulant ways in which she negotiated this. Her lineage (which we never really speak about in my family) is one that is very different from my father's. My mother's father had arrived in South Africa, not as an indentured labourer, but as a passenger Indian, a teacher of the Urdu language. And when needs must, he rapidly started a school, began training in the art of intricate wood-carving and started one of Durban's first lawn tennis clubs. They called him Samu Dada, and he was a formidable sight in any of the few photographs that I happen upon. He was tall and strapping, and always wore a white kurta pajama and a beautifully wrapped pugree on his head. His discerning feature was a fine nose, and a perfectly curled moustache above a poet's soft mouth. Often, they say that he came from the Punjab, before Partition, and ended up in Bengal to pursue his studies. In his look, I can believe this, as I can believe how he used to march around with his walking cane and his perfect command of both Urdu and English. Sadly, he died very young, and no stories of him follow. I would never know the truth.

My mother was brought up more English than the English sugar barons, who had taken my father's ancestor into indenture in the late 1800s. In her family, they took tea and scones at exactly three o'clock, and wore starched white petticoats and tennis dresses, and had a magnificent collection of Royal memorabilia. Of course, falling in love with a 'pukka' farmer's son and following him into the darkness and desolation of a family struggling to survive in a house on a hill, surrounded by sugarcane and a myriad Zulu 'kraals' (homesteads made of mud huts), had to be true love indeed. Defying class, religion and caste made a maverick out of my mother. When she used to tag me along to her bridal dressing sessions, I think she was making a maverick out of me.

Firstly, she was strongly opposed. The village elders objected to her wearing bell-bottom trousers instead of those long A-line dresses that female teachers were allowed to wear in accordance with the laws of the White ruling party. She would leave her hair untied. She even insisted on driving my father's 1974 Volkswagen Beetle, zipping around the clumpy clods of earth that stood for roads, from bridal house to bridal house, her bag of 'Town-bought' make-up and bejewelled items causing quite a stir. But brides then had so few choices, least of all in the men that were chosen for them, that they dug their heels in when it came to the person who would doll them up. They chose her. She chose me, six years old and sleepy, to be her company.

What were these weddings like? It was the late 70s. Apartheid was at its ugliest height. Gatherings of 'natives' and 'coolies' were regarded with deep suspicion. Planning a wedding meant careful and controlled thought into more than just the bland food served out of paper plates. Hindu vivaah and Muslim nikkah were not legally recognised by the Apartheid Government. For all to see, a father would give his daughter away in the religious tradition of his family in rituals that were passed down from when they came from India as labourers, and many of those rituals had to be bastardised and amended to suit the needs of the Apartheid System. Weddings were only held on Sunday mornings. This was probably the only day most people would have time away from their work. Noise, which is such a joyous component of an Indian wedding, was kept to a minimum.

Perhaps there were many other constraints that I, as a child, did not see, but the anxiety that permeated the air always whispered many things to me, as my gaze became that ever-watchful gaze of the men in the family looking out for a visit from the Special Branch (Apartheid Police).

A bride is a girl with stars in her eyes. And my mother and I were the Fairy Godmothers about to transform a cinder girl. It was with pride that I would hop out of my mother's roaring noisy Beetle, tasked with carrying bags of bobby pins and safety pins or cans of hairspray. My importance showed in the way the farm children would part like a river in tributary as I passed by, always dressed in my lovely white stockings and 'Town' dress. A flurry of women would usher my mother and I into a bedroom, where a waif-like girl sat waiting to be dressed to perfection. It didn't really matter if it were a Hindu wedding or a Muslim wedding, my mother dressed them equally well.

Of course, as I grew older, and still wielded my bags of pins and things to homes that were teeming with pre-bridal anxiety, I began to question things. Dress was something I observed and questioned first. You see, access to India for most farm families was extremely limited, and this made access to a beautiful trousseau of sarees, salwar suits and accessories very near impossible. It became a borrowing game. Red wedding sarees of course were handed down to the brides from their grandmothers' chests, smelling of mothballs. Fashion was never considered, because no one knew what the fashion was in India. There were just two ways to drape a sari. Over the shoulder forward, or over the shoulder backward. Pins would be stuck everywhere, because here was a girl, who up until that point had not even held a fragment of silk saree cloth to her body, and was now asked to walk elegantly and sit daintily, and not allow any tiny corner to slip.

Old sarees were re-purposed into stitched versions of salwar suits, which we called Punjabis. Style again, unconsidered. It was a straight tunic, drawstring pants, and fabric permitting, a rather tiny dupatta. Every little bit of excess fabric, embroidered or mirrored in intricate work, would find its way into bridesmaid dresses, flower girl dresses, ring-bearer dresses, and even backdrops for the mandap. India fabric was that precious, and it was that rare. There were of course the rich people from the Big City who could send out to India on flimsy catalogues for items long before a wedding, planning a proper trousseau, but those were not our people. Our people made do.

I was always somewhat taken aback by one particular thing amongst the Hindu brides my mother dressed. They would wear the orangey-red, or deep red or coral red sarees with as much decorum as they could muster in saree blouses that no one really knew how to sew well enough. But they always wore a white veil and tiara.

Now, I can say that this looked odd. Now I can say it because travel to India is easy, and shops bearing beautiful Indian garments dot every part of my city. Brides now have choices, and many end up looking almost like the Bollywood film stars that they dream of emulating. But, when I was growing up, it was a white veil, or nothing. And oft, it was the same gauzy white veil that had been doing its rounds amongst all the brides in the area. And that same odd tiara with a teardrop pearl that sat in that bifurcation of black hair oiled into a perfect centre path.

Photographs I look at now of cousins who were married then, and are now probably grandmothers, show me so much about the signs of the times. I see social constructs in the coy faces of brides.

I see that white veil, and I see that it was a way of looking like a White woman. I see that some of the hairstyles are not aligned with the beauty of an Indian face and delicate bindi, but rather look like the blonde girl from Abba in a red sari and a massive white veil. I see the hairstyle of Sue Ellen from Dallas on a dusky girl, powdered madly with talc to look white-skinned. I see the glaring red sindhoor, sitting so starkly against a pearl teardrop, and staining the whiteness of the veil with flecks. I even see some brides, resplendent in their grandmother's pure Kanjeevaram red sarees, wearing the oddest thing…long white satin gloves and carrying droopy bouquets. At my age now, I often wonder if there was perhaps something blue about that something borrowed.

The Muslim brides were for me perhaps the most interesting. Then I did not see it. Then, they were angels bathed in snowy clouds. Now, I lift an eyebrow. The Muslim community in Durban are all Indo-Pakistani descendants (albeit when they left India, there was no Partition). But, wanting desperately to align themselves with anything Arab, and denying vehemently their Indian (Pakistani) heritage, they would dress in trousseaus that were purely Westernised. Even today, a Muslim bride would more easily sit waiting for her nikkah to be announced decked out in dresses that are exact copies of Kate Middleton's.

With the stain of dark henna reaching high up beyond elbows, and a modicum of purdah-like net-covered skin, they cut a figure that appears like an Indian woman wanting to be a White woman. I once met a Pakistani friend, who appeared shocked at this White Dress Syndrome, telling me that in Pakistan, the brides wore reds, oranges and fuchsias. I had no explanation for this, and probably never will. I myself was shouted down when I insisted on wearing a bright pink sari to my own nikkah. It had to be a ball gown. A white one would be best. I ended up settling for the colour champagne, with a slight smile on my face...behind a not-white veil.

* * *

I guess the white veil has become something of a lens for me to view the minds of the Indian people during the duration of my conscious awareness. It has become a symbol against which I cast other larger things. Things that us Indians from India were either forced to, or subtly coerced into cutting out of our heritage with sharp scissors.

Our names.

They began to become bastardised even whilst our ancestors lay rolling about in shipholds, eating swill and dried fish.

Many of us cannot even trace our ancestry now because of the multitude of monikers that took hold of our families as they traversed the first step of being recruited (or kidnapped) whilst in India. The ship records are readily available, but frustratingly confusing. Arriving at the Ports of Bengal and Madras, the young men and very few women would be asked to state their name. I am a fiction writer, and in this license I picture a White man, pen in hand, with a British accent, barking at a dishevelled, confused seventeen-year-old boy in his Anglicised Hindi or Tamil.

'Arp kah narm kyah hair?'

Well, the result is a bunch of last names of South African Indians that make no sense at all. Kuppuswamy suddenly has his name written on his agreement document as Cooper Sammy. Shetty will now be called Chetty. And then once barked at and ill understood, if you dared say your village name instead of your 'narm', your entire lineage to this very day are known as Ramgarh, which later just becomes Ram. Your father's name becomes your last name, Sriprasad becomes Sewpersad, and well, almost every Muslim just gets a Mohammed or a Khan.

I have been fortunate in being able to trace much of my paternal lineage, due to the strong-headed nature of my Bihari great-grandmother, who although illiterate, would repeat her story to her children every night, until it became a song my father sang to me every night. She refused to let the story of her passage from India die. But I wonder now what she would have thought of how we eventually killed our names well and good.

English. That's how.

Into the 80s we careened, falling in love with our oppressor, with some madness akin to the Stockholm Syndrome. We just didn't know how to love ourselves any other way. We were a generation deprived of access to anything remotely Indian, and reacted with embarrassment if we had to say our names to the White school inspector or the White school nurse who stuck a pencil in our plaits, looking for lice.

The names took a Western transmogrification

with swift hands, but they never did reach our identity documents at the Department of Home Affairs just yet. The older folk held on tight, giving us names like Zuleikha, Charulata, Suresh and Kishore. But, at school, the tendrils of a black and white television and the gramophone records reached deep. There were many that insisted on being called Jock, Michael, Jenny and of course...Diana. Somehow, Saleem became Sam, Yacoob became Jake, Zuleikha became Julie, Paramjodhie became Jody and even my own cousin Dharmendra became Tom. My father, desperate back then for a teaching job, and wanting to fit in, packed away his beautiful name, Devraj, and was known from then on as Danny.

Many of the White hotel owners who didn't care much for the names of their at-the-ready waiters referred to any Indian as Sammy. This obviously coming from a last name of Ramasammy or Kandasammy. And then, with the strong presence of the missionaries from Europe, soon enough the Marias and Marys and Magdelenes joined the queue at the name change office at the awful brown building in Durban called 'Indian Affairs'.

It was so much easier to get a job if your White boss could actually pronounce your name. And it was often spoken of that those that persisted in their tongue-twisting names of Ghirdarielall or Rafiqullah never got too far up the tea-boy ladder. Many in my own family changed their names for a job. My father's eldest brother even forgot his proper name, after he was given a job as a fabric cutter in a factory and simply answered to Mac till the end of his days. We forgot his real name too.

Well, when Polly (Phoolmathie) married Eric (Dhaneshwar) and they had children of their own, and they saw the beauty of an English name, a brand new generation of purebred Denzels and Susans populated the landscape. My mother, still teaching then and not dressing many brides, would often joke with my father at the beginning of term how many times she would have to write down the name Denzel in the register. It was many.

* * *

Like a white net veil worn over a red saree, or an ivory satin gown sleeve that borders ornate paisley mehndi patterns, the people of Indian origin in South Africa evolved from holding tightly onto the shreds of Indian culture that they came with inside locked boxes and sewn into hemlines. But, like all migrants, or perhaps refugees the world over, evolution is the Holy Grail, the ability to blend into the current social strata. The result became the South African Indian. A mix of names formed and re-formed, and clothing worn and then not worn, and eventually as apartheid was abolished, an identity searched for and still to be found.

Now, in the year 2018, Bollywood has taken over almost everyone's lives. My Black African friends are head over heels in love with Shah Rukh Khan and Aishwarya Rai, and refuse to believe me when I tell them that they are actually lip-syncing those amazing songs. Everyone knows how to 'shava-shava' and White girls pay fortunes for bindis and henna tattoos. With the ability now to travel to India being afforded by the middle class and not just the super-rich, India is closer to us in South Africa than it ever has been. The brides no longer wear old sarees and white veils. The names of babies now have become the sweet-sounding Aaravs and Nainas.

At times I feel as African as the drum beats of a stereotype, I feel like the giraffe that frames herself against the orange-amber sunset. And then there are moments that I hear a sitar begin an alaap in my periphery and I feel as Indian as the string that is strummed. This negotiation will go on forever, this I know. In that I never did feel the need to change my name, nor wear white veils. But also in that my greatest pride is the words spoken by Nelson Mandela or a win for the South African cricket team. Perhaps this constant mercurial fluidity of identity has created a mercurial nature in me. Will I be Indian South African today, or will I be South African Indian? I am simply grateful that I am now given choices that don't require a thumbprint.

* * *

Room Number 114,
Taj Mahal Hotel,
Mumbai, India 9:15 a.m.

'Hello Daddy. Daaad. Hey, DADDDY, hello, can you hear me?'

'Kajal. Yes, it's me Kajal. Kaaa Jill...like your daughter okay, hello, remember! Good Wi-Fi, yeah... can you hear me clearly?'

'Yeah, like...Dadddy...Daadi is driving me like super crazy. I know you insisted that we bring her and Sharmila Bua along to do my wedding shopping, but seriously Dad, they are losing it. Even Mummy can't take it anymore, she's just fed up. She just runs off to the massage spa all day. '

'Yeah well, I mean Daadi is like doing weird things.'

'What do you mean what weird things, I mean you know Daadi right, she's like your mother after all, hey? Please Dad...you have to talk to her.'

'Firstly, I mean when we landed in India, she almost bent to kiss the ground. Super embarrassing! The guy who came to fetch us from the airport thought she was fainting or something. I mean everyone just like stared at her, with her tears and whatever. My India...my India...I mean like really Dad, why the heck did you have to send her to India now finally? She's super old, and can barely walk and now you make her come with us, how can I go around Andheri and Juhu to get all my bridal stuff with her slowing us down kissing every tree and chatting to like every single person in that weird mixed up Bhojpuri or whatevs...how embarrassing... Dad...even in Paheli Bridal Couture she sat there in that sicky lilac sari and spoke in that broken Hindi Bhoj...whatever and when she wanted to talk privately about prices to Sharmila Bua...I mean they spoke to each other in like Zulu...seriously...and OMG, all the ladies there just stared.'

'Okay, all right, all right I get it, whatever. But she's like driving me nuts, Dad. I am like SO sick of these stories about ancestors and ships and... Oh wait! OMG, Dadddy, she is trying to pressure Mama into taking a trip to like Patna or whatev so she can find her father's village or something. She has this wrinkled up dirty paper in her purse with the ship log or something and she keeps looking at it and crying.'

'No. Hell no! We are not going to some crazy village in boring Patna. I mean, I have so much shopping to do...you know how super stylish Aman's family is, they shop in India and Dubai like five times a year. I mean, already Aman's mother keeps talking about her Singh caste, Brahmin caste thing in her sideways language. Like imagine if he EVAAAA finds out my gran made a big deal about coming from like some place in some Bihar village. Dadddyyy...I mean like seriously, Daadi's gonna ruin my entire life the way she's behaving.'

'No, I can't put her on the phone, she took Sharmila Bua and they went out again to stand and stare at the stupid ocean which she does like a hundred times a day. I'll call you when she gets back muttering about the ships and bloody heck Kala Pani and whatevs.'

'Oh and DAD...OMG I have to tell you this...I mean OMG. Seriously. Yeah, she like took a tiny bit of soil from near Marine Drive and dumped it in a packet and she like carries this thing around with her in her old handbag all the time. YES, I mean YES. Like all the time. She says she's bringing it back to Durban. Like, think about it Dad, she's gonna get stopped at Customs or whatev if she tries to take that gross sand back to Durban. It's just creepy. You have to tell her to trash that sand before we get on the plane. NO...YOU. NO...she's your mother. You tell her. Daddly, you tell her. NO, stupid Sharmila Bua says nothing at all, just walks around with her mouth wide open, smiling at the taxi drivers. So, you speak to them. Mummy is getting super stressed.'

'Well, she already has this bottle with like a million litres of this water, she says its Gangajal or whatevs but I mean we didn't even go to the Ganges. She like bought it from this gross guy at India Gate.'

'Oh please Dad, don't be morose. Who the heck bothers to sprinkle this water on like dead people anyway? I mean, if you sprinkle India water on a live person, heck they'd be dead in no time...'

'Sorry…No. No, Dad, seriously, I'm not laughing.'

'Anyway, listen I have to go. Aman wants to FaceTime. Gotta match my gharara to his sherwani you know…yeah, the credit card's working out just fine. Oh, Dadddyy how shweeet, of course if we need I'll tell you. Gotta go. Seriously like bye bye bye. Yeah Mama has her phone. We gonna meet for brekkies…OMG if I have to see another aloo prataa again I'm gonna like puke or whatev. Ok…bye, bye.

'Oh wait, hang on Daddy…I mean it huh, you better speak to Daadi, huh. She's losing it here in India with her super emotional nonsense whatev. I mean…Daadi is behaving like this is her land or something.'

Sister Wives
Winnie, Phyllis and Jane X

In the middle of 2013 (I think it was July), one of my closest friends, Deepa,* an anti-apartheid activist and a visual artist, came to my home.

Whilst we drank pots and pots of tea, Deepa mentioned Phyllis Naidoo. Phyllis was one of the strongest woman anti-apartheid activists from South Africa. Deepa had been her friend and one of the many people who cared for her during her battle with cancer, and she remembered the struggles that Phyllis had endured.

Phyllis Naidoo, known to all activists, even those as young as me as a no-nonsense, loud-mouthed, fighter with a constant ciggie dangling from her lips and a short buzz-cut, always maintained that

*Name changed

her life was not meant for anything but the struggle against apartheid. Most idolised her and feared her in one breath. 'The world is divided into activists and assholes,' she stated in the 1970s.

I have lately come to take Phyllis' words as my own little mantra. Sometimes.

By virtue of my place in this world of forgotten anti-apartheid women, I was called to consult with one of them as a qualified therapist. I will call her Jane X, although this is not her real name. She was in an old age home, also a rampantly wild anti-apartheid activist. She had lost her marriage to the struggle, and endured much torture and loss. During my few sessions with Jane, she would lapse into silence, but then launch into rants directed at everything from the food, to the flowers, to her ex-husband.

How did I find myself in this situation? In it alone, I still probed and dwelled on it. In the immersion, I suddenly became this conduit, collecting letters and documents and stories from lost women. Old, lonely women stuck in nursing homes and low income flats. The burden of all this grief, in all its depression, melded into a burden of my own life. The only recourse was to set up a series of lenses and mirrors within me. I did not want to become one of my own characters in this slowly emerging narrative. But I became one.

For over three years, I have lived in this language of these women's words, and although writing it down in a novel that is called 'fiction' was supposed to have been my catharsis, this has not happened as yet. I am still there, honoured to have these stories, but I have had my losses as well because I chose activism over domesticity.

There are too many women to mention in this conversation, and too many layers that the mind simply boots out like afterthoughts, asking me to stop, and perhaps have a drink at the local. Let me tell you the stories. I hope I can do justice.

The Moreland Estate, the place of my birth, was where my great-grandfather was brought as a boy of eighteen, to labour on the sugarcane fields. In the years to follow, it was my grandfather who eventually saved up enough money to buy ten acres of the plantation, and this is where I grew up.

My childhood house had a large thorntree that had been there since the time of the indentured labourers, and it was tradition that the people of the Moreland Plantation would gather under this tree to discuss social and political matters. This was a tradition called 'panchayat', which in my native language, roughly translates to gossip.

When I was eight years old, I clearly recall my mother telling me of one such 'panchayat'. What was so special about this one was that, ordinarily, the women and children were allowed to linger on the fringes of the circle of men, who discussed important matters with my grandfather, who was informally designated as the leader of this gathering...but on this particular day, the children and most especially the women were told to remain indoors, and not listen in on the discussion.

My mother, who was not married to my father at the time, but used to visit the farm occasionally with her eldest cousin who had married his brother, says she stole away from the women in the kitchen and went to stare at the thorntree through a fine lace curtain that hung in the front room of our house.

All she remembers seeing was the gathering of men from my village, and there, towering above them all was a man she had never seen before. His stature struck her, his posture astounded her, but even though she could hear nothing of what he was saying, his animated hands waving wildly in the air is an image that will always remain with her. This man was Nelson Mandela.

And, many years later, my father persists in telling this story repeatedly.

He said that this tall man was running away from the White police. He said that this tall man had come to our village, because of its remoteness, asking to be hidden away, so that he could avoid arrest. My father hid his face from me when I, now an adult woman, asked him why the women and girls were instructed to stay indoors and not listen to the discussion. I still don't know the answer to this. But I feel that in all my writings, and in all my research, this is the one answer I am searching for.

Nelson Mandela, then a dangerous fugitive, with a death penalty of terrorism hanging over his head, was given a job at a petrol filling station in our village, where he hid his face behind a large cap, filling up petrol for the heavy tractors that carried burnt sugarcane to the sugar mill. My father also told me, with deep embarrassment in his eyes, that it was one of the men who had been present at the gathering under the thorntree who had eventually informed the Apartheid Special Branch of the whereabouts of Nelson Mandela. Upon hearing that he had been found out, Mandela was given a vehicle from the village, and as he was making his escape, on a bridge an hour away from my home town, he was apprehended by the police. He was charged under the Treason Trial Act (1956)—later changed to Terrorism in the infamous Rivonia Trial in 1963. He was sentenced to life imprisonment on 27 May 1963 and was sent to Robben Island with two other comrades, the founding fathers of the African National Congress. They were Ahmed Kathrada and Walter Sisulu.

A year or so after he was released on 11 February 1990, twenty-seven years after being imprisoned, Nelson Mandela visited my home town of Tongaat. It was his choice that this would be one of the first places he would visit. This time he did not have to speak under a thorntree. This time, he was given a red-carpeted event at our Town Hall. My mother insisted on going to this event. She took me along. I was seventeen. She knew that she did not have to hide herself or her daughter behind the silence of lace curtains and closed windows any longer.

The looming threat of being a girl who was pushing herself into active political awareness instead of preparing for marriage as she was expected to do, no longer bothered the elder men of my family. The marriage was non-negotiable, but in my mother's final act of freeing her daughter, she took me to this event. I saw Nelson Mandela for the first time that evening. He was beautiful—one of the most handsome men I had ever seen. He was a man in his early seventies, and to a girl of seventeen, he was still beautiful.

But, somehow, when I remember that evening, I don't remember him as much as I remember my mother. She had dressed resplendently, as if she would be given an audience with him. Her eyes shone brighter than I'd ever remembered, whilst he spoke on stage.

My mother could not contain her tears. Neither could I. When he was leaving the hall, many bodies blocked us from trying to reach him. But my mother swears to this very day, that she did indeed touch his blue shirtsleeve. I believe her.

And because I believe the fairy tale that my mother touched his sleeve, I believe in the absolute seduction of Winnie Mandela. If just seeing him could make a seventeen-year-old girl cry, and a forty-five-year-old woman behave like a seventeen-year-old, Winnie Madikizela didn't stand a chance.

* * *

No book on South Africa would be complete without talking of Nelson Mandela. But, I am not here to talk about him. Much has been said about him, and about the brotherhood of the African National Congress in articles and books *ad infinitum*. I want to talk about the Silent Sisterhood of the Struggle against Apartheid in South Africa. I agree that much has been written about the women of the struggle as well. But, much has also not been written, much has not been said. I doubt that my paltry attempts at speaking of these women will even begin to tell every narrative of every single one of these women, but in the telling of the stories of these three women, Phyllis, Jane and Mama Winnie, I hope to have created a microcosm, or perhaps cast a lens.

* * *

Winnie Madikizela was born in Bizana, a town in the Transkei area of South Africa. Her father, named Columbus, taught in a 'bush school' which is basically a school for every single age, or grade, under a tree. And like his namesake Columbus, the daughter of this one went in search of something, but ended up finding something else. Winnie went in search of love, but she founded a sisterhood of warriors.

Her mother died when she was only eight, and Winnie grew into a woman, never having a mother to teach her about being one. Strangely, the hand of fate saw Winnie and Nelson Mandela's daughters also grow up without a mother. But their mother was not dead, she was as close to it as possible, for most of their childhood.

Winnie trained to become a social worker, and was an exemplary student. She completed her social work degree in 1955. She was awarded a prestigious scholarship to study in the United States. She turned this opportunity down, and remained as a social worker in an extremely challenging environment. She was the first Black social worker at a horrible government hospital, called Baragwanath Hospital in Johannnesburg.

Winnie Madikizela was not politically inclined. As a young woman, and a very beautiful one at that, she admits to spending more time looking at fashion than at politics. But, while conducting her research dissertation, she began to look deeply into infant mortality rates amongst people of colour. She realised, to her horror, that for every 1,000 live births, there were ten infant deaths.

She began digging deeper and deeper into this, and on finding herself in controversial waters with the apartheid system, she stopped her research with the threat of losing her licence.

But Winnie's stars had aligned a direction for her that she was too young to take, yet grabbed at anyway. When Winnie Madikizela, an unassuming yet astoundingly beautiful social worker met Nelson, a handsome, (in)famous lawyer, neither of them stood a chance. It is often said that there was no force on heaven or earth that could separate them, once they laid eyes on each other at a bus stop. But, it played out that neither heaven nor earth were necessary. It was Hell that separated them.

In keeping to the facts, and not romanticising, it follows that Nelson Mandela married Winnie Madikizela on 19 June 1958. Their marriage sustained a very short honeymoon period, during which time two daughters, Zenani and Zinzi, were born in quick succession. Zenani was barely three, and Zinzi just eighteen months old when their father, Nelson, had to leave Winnie and their little home in Soweto, and go into hiding. Often, Winnie would soothe her crying babies, wondering which part of the world her husband was in, or whether he was alive or dead. She had enjoyed perhaps two disrupted years of normal domesticity and then had lost her husband to a mistress, and this mistress was the Struggle.

After Nelson was sentenced, and imprisoned, Winnie suddenly was thrust into a spotlight she could ill afford, and was ill equipped to handle. She was a very shy woman, often looking through demure lashes into camera lenses and giggling with a hand over her stunning smile. She retreated, she mourned the marriage that any young woman in love deeply craves, and she protected her children.

But, it was not in her stars to remain cloistered. The country was baying for a face—someone who would take the place of Nelson Mandela, who would show the clout and appearance to the advancing apartheid authorities, who celebrated his arrest at sunset cocktail hour on a croquet lawn.

Winnie's beautiful face became this poster. Suddenly, the coy social worker was thrust into the spotlight, cameras flashed in her face, people sang songs of praise that they had found the 'Mother of the Nation'. She smiled broadly in a photograph, one that caught her offguard, as hoards of people gathered outside her house in Vilakazi Street, Soweto. People criticised this unguarded smile. People wondered how she could smile when her husband was rotting in prison. The gossip mill had begun. Little did she realise, how vilely and rapidly this smile would be snuffed out.

It was probably the day when she was photographed with her fisted hand stuck into the air (the symbol of *Amandla*...or Power), that she now became the target.

Suddenly, the shy wife had been slapped with an arrest warrant under the Suppression of Communism Act 44 of 1950. She was asleep in her marital home, her two sleeping daughters clinging to her, when the Apartheid Police barged into her bedroom, and dragged her from her bed. Her pretty pink silk nightclothes were ridiculed and tugged at, they asked her which man she had worn this lingerie for. They prodded at her, they enjoyed looking and prodding at her admirable, tall body, and then they would leave her alone, sending warnings to her that she would pay for what her husband was doing.

Winnie found herself being banished to a small town in the then purely White Province of the Orange Free State, and placed under constant surveillance and house arrest at Brandford, a dusty, dirty town.

She immediately set to work, organising a crèche and school, but then she was rapidly stopped from this. She was allowed to return to Soweto, but it didn't end there. Desperate to break Nelson, the Apartheid Special Branch attacked Winnie. They dragged her away from her home in the middle of the night. Zinzi, screaming and grabbing onto her baby sister, ran to a neighbour's house. Winnie screamed 'Ubuntu' (an African phrase that says—what is mine is yours), and the neighbour grabbed the two baby girls, and took them into care. The two children held onto her skirts, screaming 'Mummy, Mummy, don't leave us.'

What followed was and still is a very difficult story to tell. For brevity, and perhaps sanity, I will simply state that Winnie Mandela was detained without a warrant, in solitary confinement for 491 days, and violently tortured. She was Prisoner Number 1323/69 in the Pretoria State Prison, constantly watched over by a host of wardens, the scariest of them being a woman named Brigadier Aucamp (Winnie called her Brig). In a 15 x 15 foot cell, with grey walls, a grey floor and grey ceiling, she spent out 491 days. She was refused her medication for an existing heart condition and began blacking out and getting

seriously low blood pressure. She constantly thought
of suicide. But, as she writes in her journal:

> 'I have decided I should commit suicide but to
> do it slowly to spare Nelson and the children the
> pains of knowing I did not have courage.'

Brig, as Winnie called her, used to constantly taunt
this woman inside a tiny cell, where the bright naked
light bulb was never switched off, such that Winnie
didn't know if it was day or night. Brig would tell
Winnie how well Nelson was doing, how he was
putting on weight. The screams of her daughters
taunted her too, as each day she was reminded of
those screams by the wardens. They described horrors
that the little girls were allegedly enduring, and they
hounded Winnie to believe that it was all Nelson's
fault. Winnie speaks of how she saw scrawled into the
walls, 'Joyce was here, Nondwe was here, Shanti was
here.' These were all Sister fighters, her Comrades
who had been in that miserable 15 x 15 foot coffin
before her. Their names gave her courage.

Of course, before anything, I have to mention
that Winnie Mandela, who radiantly celebrated her
eightieth birthday party in early October 2016, still
carries much shadow and controversy. She had come

out of prison an angry woman, a changed woman. Yes, she came out in rage. She went wildly against the slow and peaceful advance of the African National Congress, she was accused of murdering the young alleged police informant, Stompie Seipei, she had a torrid and much publicised affair with a much younger man, Advocate Dali Mpofu, whilst Nelson Mandela was in prison. She advocated burning the White Man to the ground. She disappointed Nelson, she was shunned by the ANC, and although she held his hand when he was released from prison and walked through the gates with him, their marriage was over. Nelson and Winnie Mandela divorced in March 1996.

Winnie never remarried. Her name was conspicuously absent from his Will after his death on 5 December 2013, and this year, after she tried to return to their ancestral home, she was barred from entering it. She continued to reside in Soweto, she became an alcoholic, lashing out with cuss-words in national newspapers that the 'ANC is wrapping themselves in silk sheets.'

She became an Evitaesque figure in Soweto, arriving in Mercedes Benz's, wearing expensive shoes and bright patterned headscarves, she took young lovers on trips on a Concorde to Paris, she shouted and she howled and she raged. She was openly compared to the other wives of the struggle, the silent graceful ones, like Albertina Sisulu who had borne her marital separation with poise. Whilst they were called graceful, Winnie was called wild. But.

Forty years after she was released from prison, a package arrived from London at Winnie's door brought by an English lawyer she didn't know. This package was a stack of documents Winnie had forgotten ever existed. This was her journal. The one she kept whilst in prison, once they allowed her use of paper and pen. She was seventy-five years old, and the memories and horror returned to the somewhat false peace this woman's soul had found.

She couldn't look at the documents. She could not bear to touch them. But, suddenly, her granddaughter died in a car accident. And a torrent was unleashed. Winnie attacked the journals, like the wolf-woman people knew her for. She pawed through them. And then finally, at the age of seventy-five, the words began to flow, the book began to write itself. Her autobiography, *491 Days: Prisoner Number 1323/69,* was published in 2013 by Ohio University Press. The world now came to know her.

And I came to read a collection of her unpublished correspondence. I love letters. I write them to many people. I even write letters to myself, and the nectar of letters from Winnie to Nelson and from Nelson to Winnie was too sweet for me to resist. Too much nectar. And, now...after all this, I can tell you why I understand Nomzamo Winnie Mandela now, as I understand my own self. Reflection and drawing intersecting lines has been my blessing and my curse.

I begin with citing a letter that Nelson wrote to Winnie, on the day she was released from her months in solitary confinement, and later from imprisonment itself (although she remained under constant state watch and interference):

> My dearest Winnie
>
> I had to wait two weeks before I could send you my warmest congratulations for serving 491...and still emerge the lively girl you are, in high spirits. From Your beloved Nelson,
>
> (1 October 1976)

In her response to him, Winnie writes:

> My darling. In a way, during the past two years, I have felt closer to you. Eating what you were

eating, and sleeping on what you sleep gave me
the satisfaction of being with you.

(26 October 1970)

I will now give a few excerpts of the letters between
Nelson and Winnie, in their apparent chronology.
Because one must remember that letters were
written, but often remained with the Special Branch,
screened, words blacked out in thick ink, and they
often were returned to sender. If they did reach the
hungry recipient, it was always a hodgepodge of
dates, a pastiche made even more confusing with the
confusion of whether it was day or night, winter or
summer, birthday or death-day:

> Dear Winnie
>
> Most people don't realise that your physical
> presence would have meant nothing to me if the
> ideals for which you have dedicated your (our)
> life have not been realised. Nothing can be as
> valuable as being part of a parcel of the formation
> of history of a country.
>
> Devotedly, Dalibunga* (5 August 1969)

*Dalibunga was Nelson Mandela's clan name, given to
him after initiation into adulthood, a practice common to
Xhosa males.

My darling Nelson

I have learned from you. How I laughed when I recalled the medical student we know. Remember the horrible green car? It refused to start. Remember the funny story of the Evangelists?

Love, Winnie (11 November 1969)

Dear Winnie,

We stand in a relationship now, not as husband and wife, but as sister and brother. In the past, I have addressed you in affectionate terms, for then I was speaking to a wife. But now, in the Freedom Struggle we are all equal, and your responsibility is as great as mine.

Hugs and kisses to the girls. Nelson (16 November 1969)

At this particular point, Winnie's responses become conspicuously absent. She retreats, and then tries again. Between Nelson and Winnie there are hundreds of letters, now found, many, I am quite certain, will never be found.

But, the striking thing is that in the few letters that I have read, Nelson's voice is asking a wife to become a sister. A comrade of the struggle. Somehow, he has admired his beautiful wife now, whilst he sits in prison planning and reading and discussing the future of the advance against the Apartheid Government.

Winnie sits alone in her house, surrounded by two children, who grab at her. Surrounded by a desperate country that grabs at her. She receives no comfort that a wife is craving from a husband. The result is that Winnie decides that the way to Nelson's heart is through his mind. She wants to win his love. She wants letters of undying love, affection, mounting passion. But, perhaps it is censorship, perhaps he just could not say it inside his loneliness, but the subtext *and* text in Nelson's letters talk of Freedom, Literature, Law and the Struggle. Slowly, Winnie begins to realise...she is no longer a wife. Not even a widow. Now, as a Comrade of the Struggle, she has become Nelson Mandela's Sister-Wife.

This is the worst place for a woman to be. Most especially a woman who is brimming with repressed passion for a man she just cannot get a hold of. Even in letters, even in blacked out sentences, she just cannot get a hold of her man. She begins to academicise herself. Do you think she will win his passion? Listen:

Dear Nelson

I still cannot believe that at last I have heard
from you, my darling. In my handwriting you
will notice the hypnotising effect your letters have
on my soul. All I have needed is a natural drug
after all. We were hardly a year together when
history deprived me of you. Your formidable
shadow, which eclipsed me, left me naked—a
young political widow.

I looked in the mirror. My hair is white, there
are bags under my eyes. At age thirty-six!

When I visited you at the Fort, do you
remember, you said, 'This is not the beauty
I married. You have become ugly.' Then you
sent me a magazine on the Reigning Beauties of
the World—the Women and the Power behind
politically successful men. I was furious. I had
taken such a lot of trouble to look nice for you
that day.

Winnie Mandela (26 October 1970)

And, herein lies the fracture. It is a complicated
fracture. I doubt that anyone who tries to dissect
letters between anyone will ever really know the full
story, least of all, these confusing letters between this
husband and wife.

* * *

What I strongly believe, is that Winnie loved her
husband and she lost him. His mistress was not
a woman in a mini-skirt that you could slap in
the street. His mistress was a large and important
purpose, and Winnie could not slap this mistress.
She had to learn the secrets of seduction from this
mistress called Freedom. And she had to transmogrify
into this mistress called Freedom. In this process,
she stopped being Nelson Mandela's wife, and when
they walked together, holding hands, out of the
prison gates the day Nelson Mandela was freed, it
was already too late. Now, a brother and a sister,
who stood with their backs together against an ugly
world suddenly turned towards each other, and saw
that their love was over.

Winnie was a woman of great and intense passion.
This passion blazed from her eyes. But, in her one
and only love, she believed that her passion was
unrequited. There is no doubt that she committed
atrocities, alleged murders, incited a country to
burn and kill, had a public extramarital affair, and
descended into alcoholism and drug abuse. My
plea for Winnie Mandela is not and never will be
academic. I am one woman who knows this, hence
my plea for Winnie Mandela is a plea to recognise

Nomzamo Mama Winnie as a broken-hearted lady who hated becoming a Sister-Wife.

In the closing chapter to her autobiography, Mama Winnie writes a prophetic warning to a South Africa that is now burning to the ground:

> I felt strongly that this journal and these letters needed to be published in this way, exactly as they were written at the time, so that my children and my grandchildren and whoever else reads them should please see to it that the country never ever degenerates to levels such as those. It is for their future. Right now, people like myself who come from that era become petrified when we see us sliding and becoming more and more like our oppressive masters. To me, that is exactly what is happening and that is what scares me.

This afternoon, 2 April 2018, in South Africa, the family of Winnie Madikizela-Mandela announced that she had passed away, peacefully in her sleep. The nation erupted in a sense of shock. No one had seen this coming, no one believed that the Iron Woman, the Mother of the Nation would go. But, with the shock and tears, the controversy begins. And I find myself carried by this tide too.

What is this furtive mourning I am doing? Why do I find myself actually spending my time defending my right to eulogise a woman who I have spent the greater part of five years researching, writing and speaking about? Because this woman is Winnie Madikizela Mandela, that's why. And my admiration for her evolved as I grew to know her many facets, through her words.

Social media assaults me. On Facebook I see someone post a well-recognised picture of a young, newly married Winnie, the coy one, with that slightly seductive smile spreading beyond the pixels that a picture can occupy. They caption it: 'Rest in Peace, Mama.' The comments below are generically R.I.P... But then, there is a reply: 'Take one for Stompie.'

And the page erupts with a bipolar wave, where there is little on it akin to eulogies or respect for the dead. I cannot help myself, I plough through Twitter, and find the same contradictions there. But, at some point as the night wears on, I stop myself, and simply breathe in the fact that a strong, wonderful human being, a woman is no more. It is as simple as that.

Somewhere in the many years of a marriage that had to be continuously consummated by ink on paper, there came a fracture in the mind of a wife.

Not a freedom fighter, nor a revolutionary, but merely a woman aching to be loved. She stops regaling him with love notes, and now matches his tone with that of the political machine that she has morphed into. She accepts his congratulatory note when she is released from the horrors of solitary confinement. She sees now, that one simple photograph of her standing outside her home in Vilakazi Street, Soweto, with her fist stuck in the air wields more active power over the people on the ground who are fast forgetting the men in jail. They are the myths that the people cannot see. She is the reality that can make the world see.

Winnie Mandela's role as a fierce fighter against the apartheid regime has and will be talked about for years to come. Her eulogies will include the good, the bad and the ugly. I have simply made a choice, and my choice is based on the lens of my own subjectivity. I believe that Winnie Mandela was a heartbroken woman, and within the loneliness and splintering of her own identity, she fought wilder and harder because not only had the apartheid regime deprived the Black people of their rights and dignity, she saw it as having deprived her of her life as a wife and a mother.

At eighty-one, she had silently slipped away, and Winnie was not a woman to silently do anything. She had never been a woman who patiently waited for Freedom and Democracy. She was a woman who made a day happen. She was that type of woman. The woman your mother warns you to never become, but applauds you when you defiantly do. She was a woman who believed in speaking her mind, and even till the latter years, she always did. She was a vociferous voice who spoke out about the state of South Africa as it currently stands. She expressed her heartbreak at how the legacy of the ANC had been sold.

In my thoughts on Winnie Mandela, I have refused deliberately to think about her controversies. These things have been dissected by the world far too many times. I simply wish to remember Mama Winnie in the frame of my own reference, I will always look at that curving hand, writing letters by candlelight—of love in a time of burning.

Rest, Mama Winnie. We'll take it from here.

References

1. Gandhi, MK. *An Autobiography or My Experiments with Truth*. Navajivan Publishing House Ahmedabad, 1927.
2. Edited. Meer, F. *The South African Gandhi: An Abstract of the Speeches and Writings of MK Gandhi*. Madiba Publishers/Gandhi Memorial Committee, Durban, South Africa, 1995.
3. Dhupelia-Mesthrie, U. *Gandhi's Prisoner? The Life of Gandhi's Son Manilal*. Kwela Books South Africa, 2004.
4. Desai, A. and Vahed, G. *Inside Indenture: A South African Story, 1860-1914*. Madiba Publishers Durban, South Africa, 2007.
5. Unpublished Letters: Family Archives. Nelson Mandela and Winnie Madikizela-Mandela.
6. Madikizela-Mandela, Winnie. *Modern African Writing: 491 Days: Prisoner Number 1323/69 (1)*. Athens, OH, US: Ohio University Press, 2014. ProQuest February. Web. 16 October 2016.

THE ARCHITECTURE OF LOSS

Zainab Priya Dala

A novel of forgiveness and reconciliation that shines light on the dark underbelly of South Africa's fight for freedom and democracy.

Estranged from her mother, who sent her away at the age of six, brilliant architect Afroze Bhana has carved out an impressive life for herself in Cape Town. But when she receives word that her mother is desperately ill, she is compelled to return to her hometown in rural Zululand to find answers about her painful childhood.

Afroze finds that her mother, Sylvie—a doctor and fierce activist during the dark days of the anti-apartheid struggle—is a shadow of her formidable self. But Sylvie has still retained her anger toward the daughter that she sent away. Somehow, she cannot draw Afroze close, even facing the looming threat of her own mortality. She remains frozen in the cottage of Afroze's childhood, cared for by the fiercely protective Halaima, a Malawian refugee. Especially painful for Afroze is the love that Sylvie showers on Bibi, Halaima's precocious daughter—love she never gave her own daughter.

A moving novel about the complexities of family ties, *The Architecture of Loss* beautifully explores the ways in which the anti-apartheid struggle—a struggle in which the roles of women have been largely overlooked—irrevocably damaged many of its unsung heroes.

Page Extent: 256 pp | Price: ₹399